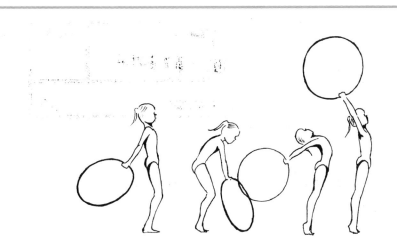

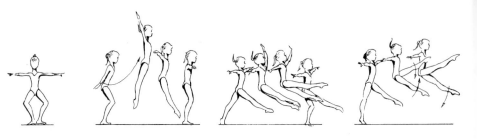

Other books of interest from A & C Black:

LEAPFROGS: *Gymnastic Activities for Juniors*
(Jim Hall)
(Available Summer 1995)

LEAPFROGS: *Games for Juniors*
(Jim Hall)
(Available Summer 1995)

Know The Game Gymnastics
(Brian Stocks and the British Amateur Gymnastics Association)

Themes for Educational Gymnastics
(Jean Williams)

Trampolining – Beginner to Competitor
(Rob Walker)

Trampolining for Coaches and Performers
(Rob Walker)

GYMNASTIC
SKILLS & GAMES

Joan Jackman
Bob Currier

A & C Black · London

Contents

First published 1992 by
A & C Black (Publishers) Ltd
35 Bedford Row, London WC1R 4JH

Reprinted 1995

© 1992 Joan Jackman & Bob Currier

ISBN 0 7136 3572 X

A CIP catalogue record for this book is available from the British Library.

Printed and bound in Great Britain by Whitstable Litho Ltd, Whitstable, Kent.

Introduction

This book is aimed at those involved in the teaching of the lower levels of gymnastics, in a school lesson or a school gym-club, in leisure centres, at play-groups, at summer-schools and at recreational level.

This approach to gymnastics is to give enjoyment and to avoid anxiety, at the same time providing sound teaching principles and progressions leading to good basic training. The book should provide ideas for teachers wishing to start children on the right path to gymnastic skills, developing fitness and introducing basic moves which when correctly mastered can lead to more advanced skills.

No apology is made for the fact that many of the movements described, games played and activities used have been taught in schools for years. The authors believe that in recent years the teaching of such skills has been neglected in schools, much apparatus is not used (sometimes due to lack of knowledge), and that now the value of such activities may be recognised again. The games and fun activities are stressed to give teachers a wide range of movements which they can call upon to increase children's enjoyment in gymnastics, while at the same time developing fitness and body awareness. Participation and performance forms the main part of this book and the activities covered are suitable for the full age ranges of under 7's and 7 to 14's. Usually the exercises described start at the younger age level, progressing to the older, more skilful gymnast. Children introduced to gymnastics in this way are on the right path to participate at more advanced levels, if that progress appeals to them.

Teachers and coaches should find this book useful for the coaching awards of the British Amateur Gymnastic Association, since it covers many of the basic skills included in the syllabus.

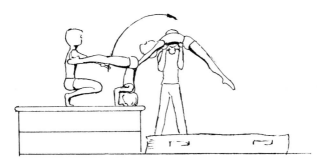

Safety in gymnastics

☐

The first factor to be considered in any school gymnastic lesson or club activity is **safety**. Any activity can be dangerous – gymnastics is not inherently dangerous – but careful precautions can eliminate most hazards.

The gymnast

1   Children should not be allowed to work in socks or shoes. Bare feet are best, but if conditions are not suited to this, gym shoes may be worn, not trainers which are too heavy and disguise the foot position and shape.

2   Clothing should permit free movement, should allow body shape to be shown and must not be so loose that garments will catch on apparatus. A leotard is ideal for girls and shorts for boys.

3   Warm clothing should be worn during warm-up and during training if the gym is cold, since a cold body can lead to muscle injury. A track suit is ideal, otherwise gym trousers and a thick jumper can be worn.

4   Jewellery must not be worn. Even a ring can catch on apparatus, injuring fingers or causing injury to other people. Pins, brooches, metal badges should not be worn.

5   Hair should be short or tied back neatly. Long hair can swing across the face and obscure vision or can swing in the teacher's face as he/she is supporting.

6   The teacher also should be suitably and neatly dressed.

The apparatus

The class must learn never to go on to the apparatus until permission has been given by the teacher. It is very tempting when apparatus has been erected to 'have a swing', but all apparatus should be checked first by the teacher for stability. Apparatus should stand evenly, fastenings should be adjusted correctly, pegs should be in on portable bars and hooks down on benches attached to wall-bars or other apparatus.

When apparatus has been placed in position the teacher should check that there are adequate landing mats, that the pieces of apparatus are not too close to each other, nor that by jumping from one piece of apparatus gymnasts are landing in the runway of another. Neither must the apparatus be too close to a wall or a window. Avoid locating a runway or descent area near a door that opens inwards.

If the class has removed items of clothing after warm-up they must be

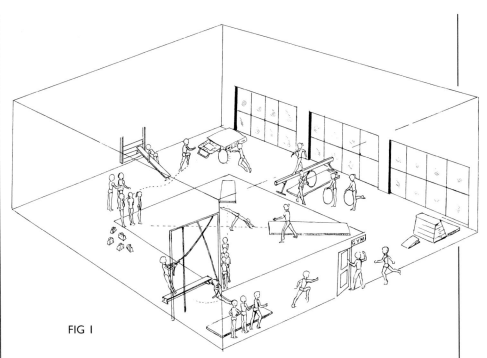

FIG 1

removed from the working area; a shoe, jumper or training bag left on the floor can be a hazard. Spot the dangers in fig. 1.

Apparatus should be checked regularly by a specialist firm.

Organisation

The class should be encouraged to enter a gym or sports hall in an orderly manner. Usually they will come in to a warm-up situation and later get out apparatus, but if they come in to find apparatus already out they must not leap on it or over it until permission has been given.

Class organisation should be such that if apparatus is being used in groups, the movement at that apparatus and back to the gymnast's place does not cross the path of any other section.

Children should be taught to move, handle and erect apparatus. They must understand how to lift it correctly, to erect it safely and to place it sensibly according to the available space.

Apparatus used should be of a suitable height for the size and ability of the gymnast or of the group using it.

Running, except as a class activity or to a specific piece of apparatus – i.e. the vault – should not be permitted in the gym. Movement around the gym and from apparatus to apparatus must be undertaken in a controlled and orderly manner.

Chewing gum in the gym should be banned and food and drink should not be brought in. During teaching, teachers should position themselves so that all work can be seen, even if they themselves are assisting pupils. If for some urgent reason pupils have to be left unsupervised, the class should sit down, or even be made to leave the room.

A well stocked first-aid box should be available.

The warm-up

It is always tempting to get on with the lesson or, in a gym-club situation, to get the apparatus out and get started, particularly when time is limited. But the warm-up is essential. It is a time to loosen up, literally to get the body warm to avoid muscle strain and injury, a time to get the class moving psychologically as a group, ready for action.

The first part of the warm-up should be used for these purposes and to improve mobility of joints and muscles, but the later part can be used for specific skill practice for those moves learned previously.

Qualifications

The teacher/coach should make every effort to keep up with modern coaching and safety methods. They should not coach beyond their qualifications and, if running a gym-club, should make sure that they are qualified for the level of work being performed and the level of club coaching responsibility they are assuming, and that they are adequately insured.

Supporting

Many moves when being performed require some form of support by the teacher or coach in the early stages. This gives children confidence and ensures their safety. It also means that the move can be broken down into stages and the gymnast guided through and corrected before the movement is performed at the correct speed and without assistance. The 'danger' period usually occurs when a new move has been learnt and is first being performed unsupported. At this time it is wise to 'shadow' the move. That is, the teacher's hands follow the pathway which they previously took when supporting but now they do not touch the gymnast, but remain only a few inches away, ready to move in if breakdown occurs.

It is generally accepted practice that there are times when children can be taught to support. This must be supervised carefully. It may be that an older child can give most valuable help in a school gym-club and gymnasts who have 'retired' often make most effective coaches.

FIG. 2

The warm-up

However short the P.E. lesson or club session, it is vital that it starts with a warm-up. A warm-up is essential to prevent injury; warm muscles perform more efficiently than cold ones. The warm-up prepares the body and also has a psychological benefit, both physiologically and mentally preparing the gymnast for the more strenuous work to follow.

Plenty of warm clothes should be worn during the warm-up; a track suit, jumper, socks and even gloves may be worn in a cold gym and should be kept on until the body is really warm. Running, jumping and skipping are the usual ways of starting a warm-up and all parts of the body must be used. Various warm-up games may be included which are enjoyable as well as effective.

Once the general body has been warmed-up and muscle temperature has increased, then specific parts of the body should be exercised, both to continue the warm-up process and to supple the various parts of the body. Skill practices may also be included here as a build-up for moves to follow later.

It is always a good idea to use music for a warm-up, even if only as background.

Activities

Gentle running with quiet, soft foot and ankle work is one of the best ways to start a lesson. This not only gets the whole class moving but is also a lesson in spatial awareness and discipline, the children making sure that they weave in and out of the others and avoid touching them. The teacher should control the class, demanding changes in speed, changes in direction and looking all the time for good foot work and posture. Running activities should last for about three minutes.

Variety can be added to the running warm-up by including other steps and jumps. During the group run, the teacher calls out for jumps to be included with the running – star jump, upward stretched jump, crouch, long or tuck. (It will be necessary to define these jumps before including them in the run.)

Other steps can also be included in the warm-up so that running can be interspersed with slipping sideways, hopping, jumping with feet together, running on hands and feet, running with short bursts of speed, skipping, running springing up and landing, and bounding steps.

Games

Not many relay races are suitable for warm-up because most of the team are waiting for the runner; games or game-like activities which have everyone moving are better for this.

I Numbers game Children run freely in the room. Teacher calls number and they must sit in a group of that number. Any left over or sitting in the wrong number perform a penalty of some sort (e.g. four star jumps, five press-ups).

2 Arithmetic groups As above but instead of calling out numbers, the groups are called in simple arithmetic, 3×2, $2+2$, $8-3$, $12 \div 2$, etc.

3 Geometry shapes Class run freely round room and, when a number and a shape are called, make that shape on mat or floor. Last one or ones left out perform a penalty but the most inventive way of forming the shape should be praised and called to demonstrate, e.g. fig. 3 – lying full length to form triangle; sitting in cross sitting, arms linked, to form circle; kneeling, feet touching, to make oblong; square; two kneeling and one on their backs to make a pyramid.

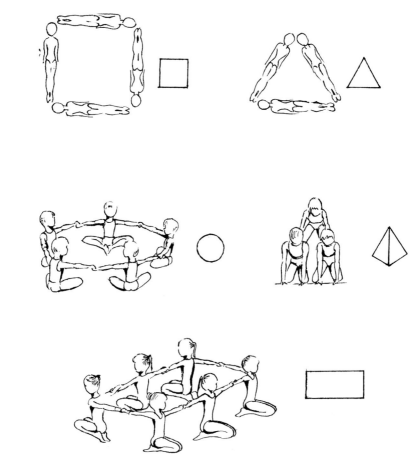

FIG. 3

4 Alphabet soup Class run, hop, skip, jump freely until a letter is called and then they must make that letter shape. It may be made standing on the floor, or against the wall, or on any apparatus which is out (fig. 4).

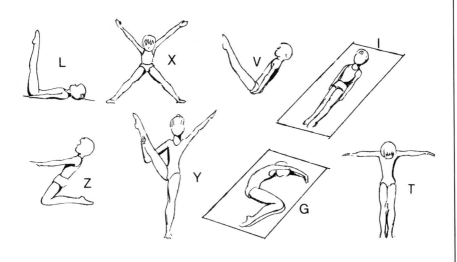

FIG. 4

5 Body parts Moving in any way round the room. When a body part is called that part of the body must touch the floor and then the gymnast must jump up quickly and resume movement round the room.

6 Body balances Free movement round the gym. On call, class balance on part of the body called and hold balance until told to resume movement. At all times in the balance the rest of the body should be held free from the floor and well stretched (fig. 5).

FIG. 5

7 Duck fighting This is done in pairs, with the children evenly matched for size/strength. They crouch down opposite each other, hands held flat in front of their chests and against the partner's hands. They try to push each other over, using flat hands only and hopping around in crouch. Hands or fingers must not be clasped, legs must not be stretched. First to fall over or put hands on the ground is out. This can be made into a champion duck fight where the winning duck hops off to find another duck, leaving the defeated duck sitting on the ground. Finally there is one undefeated duck left.

8 Cat and mouse The group is arranged in lines of five or six, holding hands down the line. The cat (wearing a coloured band) chases the mouse along the lines, which must not be broken. When the teacher calls 'Change', the lines change to face sideways and re-link hands, thus trapping the cat and allowing the mouse to escape. When the cat catches the mouse it chooses another pair (fig. 6).

FIG. 6

9 Arches tag This is played in pairs, the chasing pair wearing a band. Each pair holds hands and is chased by the banded couple. On being touched by either of the chasers, the touched pair have to face each other and hold both hands to make an arch. The caught pair must stand still and can only be released by another free pair running underneath their arch. If a pair breaks hands then that is the same as being touched and they must make an arch. If the catchers break hands then they cannot catch anyone until they have reformed (fig. 7).

10 Circle race A double circle is made, the inside team in cross sitting in front of a partner in the outer circle, who stands with legs astride. On 'Go', the inside circle crawls through the legs of the outside circle and runs clockwise round the outside of the circle. When they reach their own partner they crawl

FIG. 7

FIG. 8

in through the legs and sit (fig. 8). (Make sure they know which direction they are running in, otherwise crashes occur.)

11 Target ball tag The whole class spreads out around the room. One player, wearing a band, is the first chaser and has a fairly soft ball with which to run and chase the others. Once this player has thrown and touched another player, then the former can no longer run with the ball. The second player puts on a band and also becomes a catcher, but neither may now move when the ball is in their hands, only to chase after it and throw it. The game continues until only one player is left 'free'.

12 Star relay Four or more teams are arranged in lines in a star shape. Number 1, at the front of the team and centre of the star, has a netball and bowls it through the legs of the team to the last player, who runs with it round the outside of the star until returning to the team. This clockwise run is three-quarters of the circle; the player then cuts in to the front of the team. This player bowls the ball back through the legs to the last player who again runs

FIG. 9

round the circle (fig. 9). The race finishes when the whole team is back as they started with the ball with the front player.

13 Collect relay Teams are arranged between two lines with the first player behind the back line and the others spaced down the room between the lines. Four skittles mark the back corners of each team's running area. Number 1 starts off running round the back left skittle, down to the front left, across in front of the team to the front right, then back to the back right, across the back line and down to the next player in the line. Player 1 holds player 2's waist from behind, then they both run forwards, front left, across to the front right, down to the back right, across the line and down to pick up player 3 (fig. 10). This continues until the last player brings them back to the starting position.

14 End ball There are several different versions of this game but this is our favourite. It may be played on a badminton or netball court, where the centre court is a neutral zone, or in an area marked in two halves with tramlines at the back of each end (fig. 11). The game starts with two teams, each in their own half. A bounce is taken in the middle between two players. Whoever gets the ball may, from their own half, throw at once at any member of the opposite team. If the ball is caught or picked up, the game continues with the player with the ball passing it or aiming at the other team. If a player is hit or drops the ball then they are 'out'. But they have not finished playing; they move to the back of the opponent's team and any ball which comes through to them or is passed overhead to them they may use to attack the other team from the rear. The game continues until all the players from one team are 'out'. Players may catch the ball, pick it up, run with it, pass it. Anyone still 'in' may go into the neutral zone to fetch a ball and may throw from there, but once 'out' they must remain in the back tramlines and throw from there. No other player may go into the back tramlines once there is an opponent there. This may take too long as a warm-up game if there are many players.

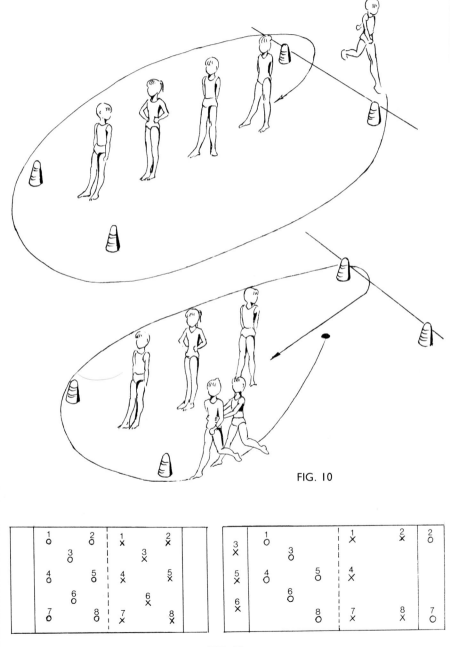

FIG. 10

FIG. 11

Developing mobility and strength

☐

Most gymnastic activities require mobility or strength; training for these should be included in every lesson or gym-club session. Generally, it is preferable for mobility exercises to come at the start of the class and strength at the end but, where time is limited, some doubling up can take place. Thus warm-up activities can also be suppling, some skill training before an activity can also involve strength work and game-like activities can enhance either mobility or strength training. Duck fighting, described in warm-up, is a good leg strengthener; many of the warm-up games, such as alphabet soup or body part balances, are also good for mobility.

Mobility training

▓ SHOULDERS

1   Windmills. Standing with feet slightly astride, both arms swinging in circles backwards, left and right arms following each other. The arms should circle close to the ears and the body, with head held erect.

2   As above, with arms turning either backwards or forwards, running gently round the room at the same time.

3   Holding a stick or towel in front of the body, the arms swing up and over until the stick is behind the body. This is then repeated forwards. At all times the arms must be kept straight. Gradually, as the shoulders become more mobile, the hands can be placed closer together (fig. 12a).

4   Kneel on the ground, bottom high, and push the shoulders to the ground, arms straight on the floor in front of the head (fig. 12b).

FIG. 12a   FIG. 12b

▪ *WRISTS AND HANDS*

1 While running and warming-up, circle and shake the wrists and hands.

2 Sea-lions. Kneel with hands and knees on the ground, hands shoulder width apart and flat on the floor. Lift the knees from the floor, seat high, then walk forwards with the hands and drag the feet behind, legs straight, dragging the feet along on their top surface. (Wear socks for safety.)

▪ *SPINE*

Care must be taken when exercising the spine but, in general, the aim should be to maintain natural mobility and to improve those areas found to be stiff.

1 Happy cat – angry cat. Kneeling on all fours, hollow the back, keeping the head high – happy cat – and then humping the back, head dropping down – angry cat.

2 Body bending sideways. With feet slightly apart, reach the arms above the head, keeping them close to the ears, and then bend the upper part of the body alternately left and right. The body must not twist and the head should be kept up and between the arms all the time (fig. 13).

FIG. 13

3 Arch and curl. Sitting with knees bent and feet flat on the floor, with arms above the head, arch the body backwards, then bring the arms down, curl the back forwards and clasp the hands round the shins, head to the knees (fig. 14).

FIG. 14

4 Trunk circling. Standing with legs apart and arms stretched above the head, circle the body with as big a circle as possible, reaching forwards, sideways, backwards, sideways and forwards, first to the left and then to the right.

▨ *HIPS*

I All leg swinging exercises. Standing with feet together, one hand supported at shoulder height on wall-bar, box-top etc, swing the outside leg forwards, back to the start, sideways, return, backwards, return. At all times the back must be kept straight, hips forwards and not twisted, head up and legs straight, feet and ankles stretched. Turn and repeat the other side.

2 Squat, knees turned out, arms at shoulder height. Alternately stretch left and right legs sideways. Keeping the body upright and hips low, transfer the weight to the stretched leg (fig. 15).

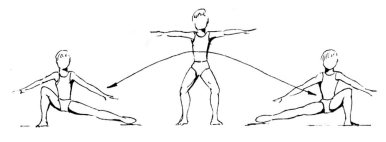

FIG. 15

3 Sit well forwards on the bottom, soles of the feet pressed flat together. Hold the feet with the hands and gently press the knees down towards the floor, bouncing them up and down with small movements.

4 Sitting on the floor with legs astride and feet and ankles well stretched, bend the trunk to alternate sides, pressing the chest to the knees.

▨ *HAMSTRINGS*

These muscles run from the pelvis down the back of the legs to below the knee-joint.

I Caterpillar walk. Stand with flat feet, place hands flat on the floor, well ahead of the feet. With small steps bring feet to the hands, keeping knees straight and getting the bottom high. When feet are as close as possible to hands, walk hands forwards, still with them placed flat (fig. 16).

FIG. 16

2   Lie flat on the back with one leg raised straight in the air. Keeping the leg stretched, sit up enough to grasp round the lower leg and try to pull the leg to the chest (fig. 17).

FIG. 17

3   Sit in long sitting on the floor, legs stretched and together. Bend the body forwards, gently bouncing the chest to the knees. To make this exercise stronger, turn the feet upwards towards the body.

Strength training

Exercises and many types of apparatus work can be used to strengthen the body; some strength work should appear in every lesson, such as rope climbing or bar work. But there should also be specific strength training to ensure that all parts of the body receive this conditioning. Strength training is best done for a time at the end of each session.

Muscles work in two ways – dynamically or statically – and they have an origin and an insertion. Movement is usually brought about by the insertion moving closer to the origin – as in bending the arm. This is working concentrically – the muscle is shortened or contracted as in bringing the lower arm towards the upper, bending at the elbow. Here the insertion on the lower arm moves towards the origin on the upper arm and shoulder girdle.

When stretching the arm (moving insertion away from origin), the flexor muscles work eccentrically; when muscles contract without movement taking place (i.e. hanging, with bent arms), the elbow flexors are working statically.

In many exercises all three types of muscle action may take place. For example, in push-ups the arm extensors work concentrically to push the body up, hold the position with static muscle action and then control the lowering to the ground eccentrically.

▓ *GAMES AND ACTIVITIES*

Animal walks
(These could also be used in warm-up)

I   *Seal walk*. (Best done in socks, although in general socks alone should not be worn in the gym.) This strengthens wrists and shoulders but is also important for keeping good body tension. The gymnast walks on all fours but with the feet sliding on their top surface, arms straight and body weight well forwards. Arms are shoulder width apart and hands are flat and well turned out. The body must be kept tight and straight. Take ten steps forwards with hands turned out, then ten steps with hands turned in (fig. 18).

2   *Chicken walk*. Strengthens calf muscles and Achilles tendon. In crouch position, bottom kept well down and tucked in, hold the back of the heels with each hand and then walk forwards with tiny steps (fig. 19).

3   *Frog hops*. Leg strengthening. From a crouch position, jump forwards and upwards with full stretch, arms high above the head, then immediately return to crouch (fig. 20).

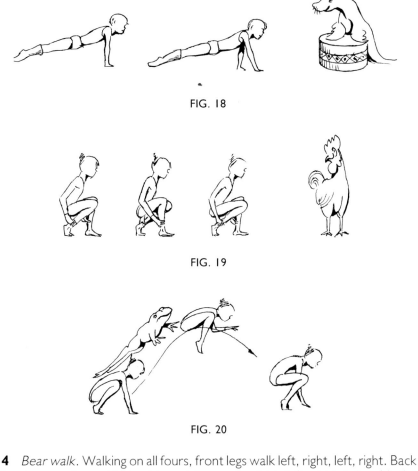

FIG. 18

FIG. 19

FIG. 20

4   *Bear walk*. Walking on all fours, front legs walk left, right, left, right. Back legs bounce from side to side and forwards, right, left, right, left, with the legs straight and straddled (fig. 21).

5   *Running apes*. On all fours, walking on alternate hands, knuckles under, jumping feet together (fig. 22).

6   *Elephant walk*. Walking on hands and feet, left arm and left leg move forwards, followed by right arm and leg (fig. 23).

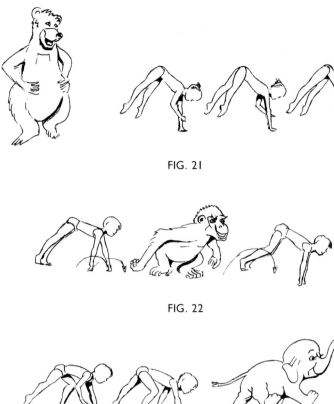

FIG. 21

FIG. 22

FIG. 23

7 *Wriggly worm.* Strengthens the muscles of the trunk. Lying on the floor, moving without hands or feet on floor (fig. 24).

8 *Bunny jumps.* Hands and feet on the floor, jumping with tail high in the air.

9 *Duck walk.* Crouch position, hands on hips, right leg swings straight to the side, then forwards (still straight) and weight transfers to the right foot (fig. 25). Repeat left.

10 *Kangaroo leaps.* Front paws held up in front of chest, large strong leaps, legs together (fig. 26).

FIG. 24

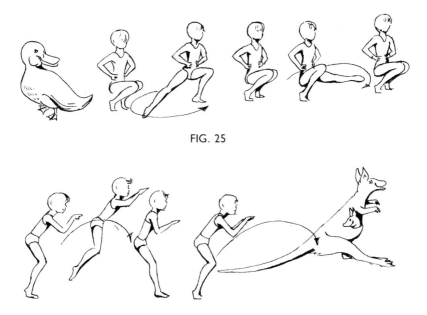

FIG. 25

FIG. 26

Relay races

1 Simple relay races can be devised using the animal walks, e.g. each relay runner doing a different 'walk', or three frogs and three chickens, or coach calls a number and a walk – No. 4 frog, No. I snake, etc.

2 Arch and ladder relay. This combines press-ups with jumps. On 'Go' all the team except No. I make an arch by doing a press-up. I runs and crawls down the line to the back, crawling under every arch. As the runner passes under the arch the team changes to lie flat (ladders). When the runners reach

FIG. 27

the end they turn and run back over the ladder rungs. When they reach their place they make a rung. 2 goes forwards over 1's rung, who then immediately makes an arch. 2 turns and runs back under all the arches, returning over the rungs to their own place to make a rung. 3 runs over the rungs to the front, back under the arches and returns over the rungs (fig. 27).

Circuits

There are many different ways of organising a circuit, e.g. so that everyone does the same number of repetitions at each apparatus station, so that everyone spends the same amount of time at each station, or so that each gymnast sets and then improves the number of repetitions at each piece within a total time.

I Circuit game – 'control'. A good circuit game can be organised in a number of small teams, three or four to a team. Team A is the 'control' and they control the time spent at the first piece. They have a task to perform, i.e. shoot baskets, or all throw and catch a ball against a wall, or all climb to the top of the wall-bars and down. Team B does as many burpees as possible.

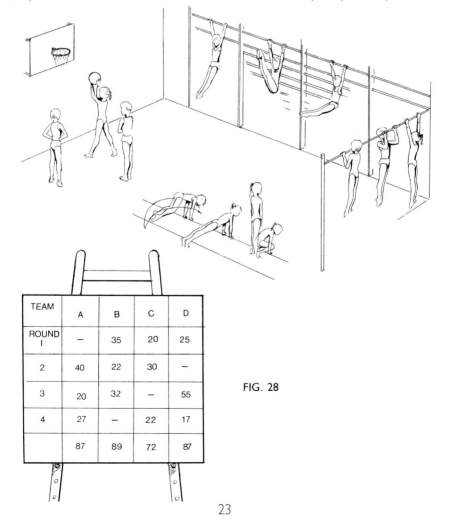

TEAM	A	B	C	D
ROUND 1	–	35	20	25
2	40	22	30	–
3	20	32	–	55
4	27	–	22	17
	87	89	72	87

FIG. 28

(Crouch position, legs jumped out and back between hands; good for legs and cardio-vascular endurance.) Team C performs pulls up to chin on bar. (Beneficial to arms.) Team D performs hangs on bar and leg lifts. (Good for abdominals and hip flexors.)

Each team records its total until team A shouts 'Stop', having reached its target. Each team then moves on one station: team A to burpees, B to chins, C to leg lifts, D to control. Scores are added to previous total (first score for A team.) This repeats until A are back at the beginning. The grand total scores win. These exercises can be varied to suit required strengths.

2 Endurance-timed repetitions. Two gymnasts at each station. Coach times 30 seconds at each station, allows 5 seconds run between stations, then starts the 30 second count again. Each gymnast keeps their personal total. Stations involve:

(a)   stride jumps on and off bench (beneficial to legs)
(b)   sit-ups, elbows to knee (abdomen)
(c)   lying on stomach, leg and arm lifts (trunk)
(d)   handstands against wall-bars, arms bend and stretch
(e)   rope climb to touch a certain height mark; jump off and repeat. (To make more difficult, climb with arms only.)

Artistic gymnastic skills

Floor work

Floor work is the basis of most gymnastic exercise and needs to be well taught at simple levels in order to form a good foundation for the more advanced skills to follow and for when the moves are transferred to other apparatus, such as the beam or vault. When the basic floor skills have been developed, creativity can play its part in the work shown, but it is important that skills are well performed with good technique before being put into sequences or transferred to apparatus.

The approach in this section of the book is based on the belief that teachers and coaches need to help the gymnast to understand and acquire simple skills. It is recognised that a school class will contain pupils with a wide variety of ability, strength, suppleness, size and ambition. The school club will probably develop some selection and increased expectation of achievement, while the gym-club will vary from recreational to competitive gymnasts. But all must have the opportunity to be taught basic skills and the secondary school teacher will be delighted if the class of primary children enter the senior school with this good grounding.

If gymnastics is to form a worthwhile part of the new curriculum development, an understanding of artistic gymnastics will be essential for child and teacher.

Safety At all times it must be recognised that safety is imperative and the teacher/coach is responsible for providing a safe atmosphere. Children should not be taught beyond their capabilities. This does not mean that they cannot progress but the varying potential for success among a group of children must be acknowledged; not all will achieve a front somersault, but all children enjoy success and for some a good forward roll will represent progression *and* success.

If teachers follow sound and tried methods of progression, provide a safe gymnastic environment, maintain an ordered, disciplined class, then the following activities are within reach of most children if taught sensitively and to the age group and gymnastic background of the pupils.

Running, springing and jumping

Running, springing and jumping all form an essential part of gymnastics. Many jumps are included in other parts of this book, in warm-up, vaulting, rhythmic, bench work and strength training. But because they are an essential part of floor work and the construction of sequences, some ideas are included here.

Running is a key element in all gymnastic activity and can take several forms. Sprinting is crucial for vaulting, soft running steps may be included in sequences, endurance running may be used in strength training, and running, dodging, stopping and sprinting will be used in games. Running is also essential for jumping and every lesson should include some training, which can form a useful part of warm-up and body preparation.

Children should be able to run softly, with changes of speed and direction, and make good use of space, avoiding other gymnasts and holding good posture throughout. Good posture is central to running, though the body will lean slightly forwards to increase speed. Shoulders should be relaxed. Bodyweight must be on the balls of the feet, with the toes turned out slightly and a strong arm action should accompany the legs. Feet and legs must lift straight and clear from the floor, showing no swinging out from the knees or rolling of the body. Running, especially for vault or into strong acrobatic moves, must be in a straight line. A run-up for an explosive action such as vault starts slowly and then accelerates. Many gymnasts, particularly girls, run with arms swinging across the body; this slows the running action and impedes what should be a smooth rhythm. There should be a good lift of the knees and the legs should remain parallel with each other.

Skipping steps, showing stretched feet and ankles, both on the spot and travelling, are simple but need to be well taught. Attention should be paid to lightness, clean lifting of the feet from the floor, and knees coming up in front of the body (not with the foot lifted up behind). Extension should be shown through the feet and ankles and there must be resilient movement from the floor.

Running, changing to other steps, such as side slipping, skipping, trotting and bouncing on the spot, are all preparation for more specific jumps. With each change the children should feel and recognise the differences in leg action necessary to define the movements clearly.

Jumps from one foot to the other (leap), jumps from two feet to two feet (double beat) and from one foot to two (single take-off) need to be clearly defined and practised. Using circles on the floor or hoops, experiment with jumps into and out of the circles, illustrating the one and two foot take-offs and landings.

Vary the acceleration into jumps – a short approach, maximum three steps into a high jump, longer run, greater acceleration into a long leap. Run a few steps, jump, land and hold a balance, feet slightly turned out, with 'give' in the knees, hips and ankles. Demonstrate the difference in balance from an upward jump and from a long jump, when the forward momentum is greater, making landing control more difficult.

Ballet training is essential for good floor work, but few school gymnasts will have received much ballet training and, in fact, some gymnasts who have trained in ballet appear to have an exaggerated turn-out of the feet, often a handicap. But the basic *plié* position is vital for good jumping, both for take-off and landing. With the feet in first ballet position, heels together and feet turned out, the gymnast bends at the knees, turning the knees outwards; this prepares for a good upward thrust. The turn outwards of the knees comes from the hip-joint and the angle between the feet should be about 90 degrees. Good posture must be maintained throughout the jump. On landing the weight returns, first to the balls of the feet, then to the heels, with the knees and hips bending slightly; this absorbs the shock of landing and enhances lightness and quietness. The body should maintain good posture and control throughout, not leaning forwards on landing, which will lead to lack of balance and spoil the body line.

Small children can show many changes of shape with jumps without formal names being used. A few steps into an upward jump, a wide jump, a long jump and a straight jump, will produce many changes of shape.

The gymnast must show a good arm swing to aid the jumps. The arm swing comes from just behind the line of the body; thrust is created by a simultaneous straightening of hip, knee and ankle-joints with a forward and upward swing of the arms. However, the arms should **not** be thrown back behind the level of the ears, which will lead to a hollowing of the body; rather the body should be slightly piked.

Posture must be maintained throughout all jumps – head up, shoulders relaxed, full extension shown at start and finish, whatever shapes may be required during the move. In floor sequences and beam work it is important to introduce a variety of jumps and leaps. A jump is usually a move from two feet to two feet, a leap is from one foot to the other and a hop is from one foot to the same foot.

Stretch jump   The stretched or straight jump is the most basic jump, but is often badly performed. It is an upward jump on the spot, with arms stretched above the head, exhibiting good height and extension. At full height the body shows a slight hollow and then as the landing is reached, the legs are slightly forwards in a pike position.

Cabriole jump   This is an extended jump in which the legs are extended forwards and beat together in the air, one under the other. The under leg beats the upper leg, pushing it even higher.

Scissor kick   This is also sometimes called a 'hitch kick'. Step forwards with one foot, kicking the other in the air. As the first foot begins to come down, the second leg swings up, passing the other in the air and landing on the first, then the second leg.

Change leg split leap   A split leap is usually made after two or three running steps in order to increase momentum for increased height and length. This can also be performed with a change of leg in the air. Take-off is from one leg into a full split position in the air; then, after the full split has been shown, the other leg swings forwards to show splits, with the second leg in front.

Ring leap   This is a jump off one foot, with an extended front leg and the back leg swinging backwards and upwards with the rear foot, towards the head.

Hops These give useful variety to an exercise since many shapes can be shown by varying the arm or leg positions. The gymnast takes off from one foot and lands on the same, lifting the free leg in front. The free leg may be lifted high or low, bent or straight. Arms may be in opposition – left arm forwards with right leg or vice versa. The raised leg may be taken to the side or to the back, or a turn may be introduced.

Turning jumps Turning jumps (as shown in the BAGA Awards), half turns and full turns may appear easy but are difficult to perform well while maintaining good posture and balance. The arm action is essential to performing any turning moves.

From standing, with a slight bend at the knees and ankles, an upward jump is made. At the same time the arms are thrown up strongly. To make the half turn, the head is turned in the direction of the twist. Turning left, the head looks over the left shoulder, the right arm moves across in front of the head and the arms then stay close together, stretched above the head, until the half turn is complete. Landing must be controlled, in balance and from the high extended position; there must be a slight bending of the knees, hips and ankles on landing. The full turning jump is similar but requires greater height in order to complete the greater turn. Care must be taken to keep good body tension, otherwise balance will be lost on landing (fig. 29).

FIG. 29

FIG. 29

◼ FUN JUMPS

Bear dancing   Tuck jumps on the spot with one leg tucked and the other stretched. Alternate legs. Try five jumps on each leg, five on the left then five on the right.

Crayfish jumping   The crayfish jumps backwards to avoid danger. In the gym the children move backwards, moving one hand then the other, then jump both feet together, **backwards**. This can also be used as a relay race. The teams line up behind a line and then the first in each line jumps backwards until all four crayfish feet are in a circle drawn on the ground in front of the team. Then the runner runs back to touch the next one in the line. (It is surprisingly difficult to jump backwards in a straight line.)

Running and jumping relay   Two teams are arranged, sitting in two lines facing each other across the gym, with room to run behind them. Four skittles mark the shape of the racing track. Number I in each team (the runner at the back end of the line) has a relay baton. The I's run round the back skittle, down the centre of the room, between the two teams and cross over with each other. They then run behind the front skittle and up behind the opposing team. At the back of the room they again pass behind the skittle, down the middle of the room, cross over, behind the skittle at the front of their own team and, completing the figure of eight which they have run, they hand over the baton to the next one in the line (fig. 30).

This is a very exciting race involving fast sprinting down the long runs and good foot work round the corners. It can be made more difficult by placing an obstacle in the centre run which must be jumped over, but this must be easy to knock over as the children are running at full speed and at the same time may be racing their opponent for the lead position at the centre spot. A runner knocking over a skittle or the centre jump is penalised by having to stop and replace it.

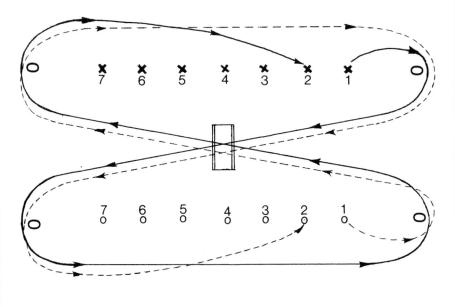

FIG. 30

Thirty second run or jump relay Three or four teams are arranged behind a line and, one at a time, have thirty seconds to see how many times they can run up and down, crossing over a line at each end of the gym. Each runner's score is added to make a team total. Variety can be introduced to this by making the team perform a variety of jumps instead of running.

Rolls

There are many basic rolls in gymnastics and from these the creative, well-prepared gymnast can develop many other shapes, starting and finishing positions, transfer the rolls to other apparatus, and include them in sequences. Rolls form an important part of rhythmic gymnastics, sports acrobatics and the initial shape for somersault moves.

With the recent growth of soft play apparatus and pre-school programmes of gymnastics (such as mother and child classes and play groups), small children are given the confidence to start rolls and other moves. Soft play apparatus, giving an inclined surface for learning, is the easiest way to start rolls with very young children. But much of normal apparatus can be adapted safely, e.g. a springboard covered with a mat will provide a good, gentle incline (fig. 31).

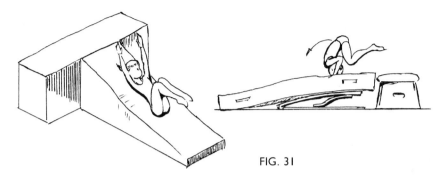

FIG. 31

■ FORWARD ROLL

The very young child may find it easiest to do the forward roll from straddle standing, leaning forwards, tucking in the head and pushing forwards, but will probably not be able to stand up after the roll (fig. 32).

For slightly older children the roll is best taught from crouch position. (Many will try to start from kneeling.) From crouch, the arms reach forwards, the weight is taken on the hands, the seat is lifted, the head is well tucked in so that contact with the ground is made with the back of the head and neck, not with the top of the head. The legs are kept straight so as to generate a strong push from the feet and the arms bend so as to provide a change of balance, leading to a forward rolling movement. The body is kept in a tight tuck position, then by reaching forwards with the arms and shifting the bodyweight forwards, the child will learn to move forwards into crouch and later to stand without touching the floor again and without another push from the hands (fig. 33). At first the child may land sitting, kneeling or with one

FIG. 32

FIG. 33

leg tucked in; practice on an incline will help to achieve the crouch position. Later the roll may be taken to standing.

▨ *BACKWARD ROLL*

Certainly children will find the backward roll more difficult than the forward and again practice down an inclined surface such as soft play, a springboard with a mat, or a double bench covered with mats, will help progress.

An early practice is to rock the body back and forwards while lying curled up on the back, trying to get well back to the shoulders. One of the most common faults is to place the hands on the floor facing away from the feet or facing towards each other; the arms collapse on to one or both elbows, resulting in a lack of strength and a crooked, collapsed roll.

Small children can be shown the rabbit crouch, with their hands up like a rabbit's ears. As they rock back, the ears are kept by the head and as they reach the back roll position, the fingers will be pointing forwards towards the feet, and a strong push can be given from the floor.

A strong push from the floor and a high lift of the hips will enable the body to move back over the head, which is the difficult part of the body to clear. (If children find this difficult at first, it may be permitted to turn the head to one side and roll over the shoulder rather than the head.) But once the timing is correct, the strong push should enable them to lift over the head to land on the feet. As the roll improves, the gymnast should aim to achieve a high lift of the hips; this will help with the more difficult move of backward roll to handstand.

Rolls can lead to some of the most creative shapes in gymnastics and once the basic forward and backward rolls can be performed effectively, many other shapes can be explored by varying the starting and finishing positions and the body shapes.

▨ *FUN ROLLS*

Here are a number of rolls to try out. Once a class has tried some of these they will be able to think up many more.

I Forward or backward rolls to straddle standing (fig. 34).

2 Rolls to come up to kneeling on one leg, the other leg stretched sideways (fig. 35).

3 Backward roll to front lying (fig. 36).

4 Forward roll to back lying (fig. 37).

5 Roll back to a shoulder-stand; then with a small swivel of the hips, bring the legs down to kneeling over one shoulder (fig. 38).

6 From standing, lean forwards and roll forwards without putting the hands on the floor (fig. 39). (Free forward roll.)

7 Log roll. Lying full length on the mat, the body rolls over, side, face, side

FIG. 34

FIG. 35

FIG.36

FIG. 37

FIG. 38

FIG. 39

and back. (It is good tension training to have one child attempting to roll their partner over while the log lies stretched and still but tries to resist being turned – fig. 40.)

8 Arabesque balance into a free forward roll (fig. 41).

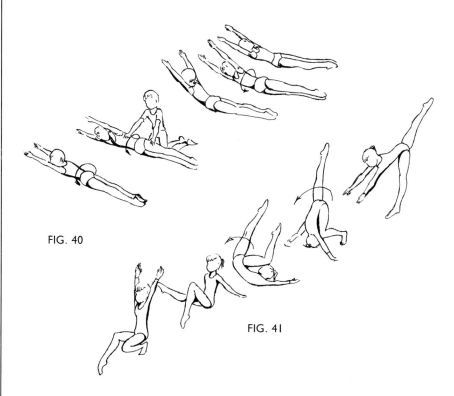

FIG. 40

FIG. 41

9 Roll back to a shoulder-stand and then lower the whole body, stretched, to front lying (fig. 42).

10 From kneeling, roll sideways to one hip, then to a shoulder-stand and down to the second hip (fig. 43).

11 Straddle sit roll (fig. 44). (Circle roll or teddy bear roll.)

12 Rolls with different shapes. Practise a shoulder-balance and then set each group to find three different ways of getting to this shape from a variety of starting positions. From a shoulder-balance, find as many ways as possible of getting out of the balance. Practise rolls at different speeds: work out which shape leads to the fastest roll, which shapes are the slowest.

13 Rolls with small apparatus. Work in groups with small apparatus and combine rolls with apparatus. Roll through a hoop held by a partner. Dive to roll over a large ball. Roll over a low rope. Find ways of rolling over a partner (fig. 45).

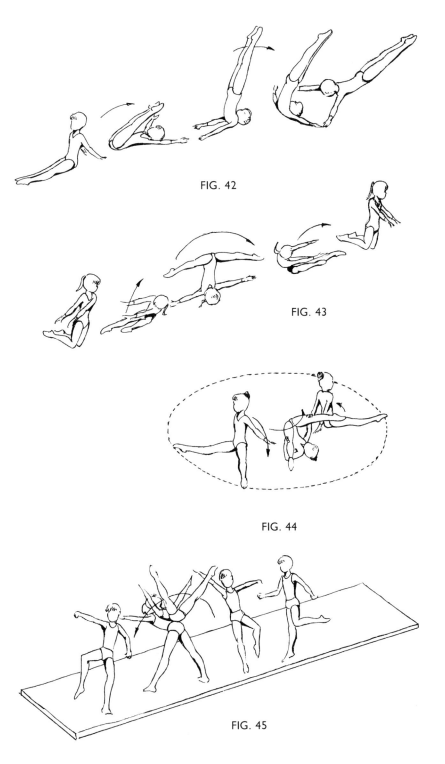

FIG. 42

FIG. 43

FIG. 44

FIG. 45

14 Combine rolls with jumps: forward rolls into high upward jumps; backward rolls into a straddle jump; high jumps, land and roll (fig. 46); rolls in sequence with jumps.

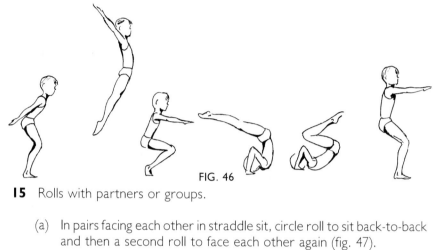

FIG. 46

15 Rolls with partners or groups.

(a) In pairs facing each other in straddle sit, circle roll to sit back-to-back and then a second roll to face each other again (fig. 47).

(b) *Tank rolls*. One partner lies on the back, knees bent, feet flat on the floor. Partner stands astride, holding the ankles of the other on the floor. The standing partner rolls forwards slowly, leaving the legs stretched behind for as long as possible. The partner on the floor grasps the ankles of the rolling gymnast and as they both roll forwards, is pulled up and in turn rolls forwards over the partner (fig. 48).

FIG. 47

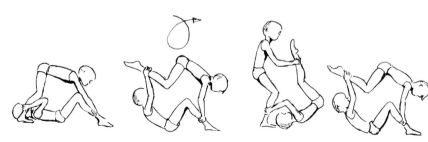

FIG. 48

(c) *Synchronised rolls in fours.* This can be performed on a normal gym mat. Four gymnasts stand one at each end of the mat, one at each side. The gymnasts are arranged so that they are opposite a space. First the gymnasts at each side roll to the opposite side into the space, then jump up and jump turn to face the mat again. Next the two gymnasts at the ends of the mat roll to change places and jump turn ready to repeat. Repeat, 1 & 2, 3 & 4. This can become faster and faster but must stop before giddiness sets in. It is possible to do this with backward rolls but it is more difficult.

Balances

▓ *HEADSTAND*

To begin learning the headstand it is as well to start with a partner. On a mat, the gymnast positions the head and hands on the floor to form an equilateral triangle, hands slightly wider than shoulder width apart (fig. 49). The forehead, not the top of the head, should be placed on the floor. The weight is taken on the forehead and, with a single foot take-off, the legs are lifted to a bent-knee headstand. The arms are kept bent, hands and wrists steady on the floor. The partner supports the lower back until balance is established, then gradually releases (fig. 50).

The second stage of the headstand is to try a straight stand. The same triangular start position is made and then, on the toes, the feet walk towards the hands and slowly lift to a straight-legged headstand.

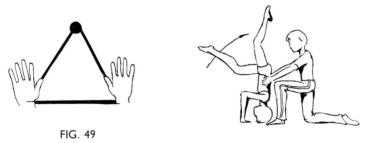

FIG. 49

FIG. 50

▓ *FUN HEADSTANDS*

Try different leg shapes while holding the headstand – bent legs, stag, straddle, one leg to the side, legs forward, etc (fig. 51). Balance on the head and, using the hands on the floor, beside the head, circle the body round on the head (fig. 52).

Chinese headstand   Balance on the head with bent knees; but instead of having the legs bent and free, lower them to rest elbows on the knees (fig. 53*a*). This is quite a steady balance and many children find it easier than an ordinary headstand and can hold it for a longer time.

Cochin China stand   Like a Chinese headstand, but instead of the head being on the floor, it is lifted forwards as the weight is supported on hands,

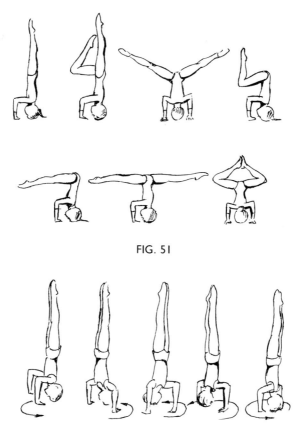

FIG. 51

FIG. 52

arms and elbows bent, and knees pushing against the elbows. The position is reached from crouch – the head is not placed first on the ground (fig. 53*b*).

Roman bridge   This bridge is made from the head to the feet (fig. 53*c*). The feet may be on the floor or may be supported on a bench or low box-top. The hands may be on the floor beside the body but this is also used as a weight-training exercise, when the bridge is held and the arms used to raise and lower barbells.

The headstand may be held with one hand on the floor and the other on low apparatus such as a box-top or low wall-bar.

FIG. 53*a*   FIG. 53*b*   FIG. 53*c*

▓ *HANDSTAND*

The handstand is probably the most important gymnastic move since it is essential for good floor, bar, beam, rings and vault work. When the handstand is correctly performed the body should be held inverted, weight on the hands, and a straight body position held, i.e. such as where an imaginary line would pass through ankle, knee, hip, shoulder and wrist. Strong arms and shoulders, good body tension and correct hand positioning should lead to a straight, stretched body position and not the banana shape so often seen (fig. 54).

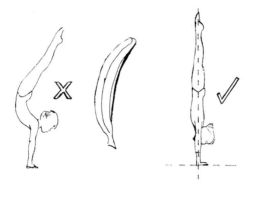

FIG. 54

At first the small child should learn by kneeling, placing the hands (fingers facing forwards on the floor) shoulder width apart, and stretching the legs, lifting the bottom high. Then one leg should be lifted up, high and straight, with the second leg still on the floor but beginning to feel that it too will be lifted. This should be carried out a number of times with each leg. Repeat, but with the second leg swinging up before the first has grounded.

All practices where the weight is taken over the hands, such as high bunny jumps, cat spring and donkey kick, are beneficial for handstands (fig. 55).

At first when attempting the full handstand, the child will need support. Early support should come from the coach facing the gymnast and holding the child by the hips, keeping the head low to avoid being kicked in the face.

From a stretched standing position, arms raised above the head, the child takes a long lunge step towards the coach, placing the hands flat on the floor, fingers slightly spread and hands shoulder width apart. The back leg then swings up straight, the weight moves over the shoulders, the arms are straight, then the second leg swings up to join the first. The support can then move the hands up to the ankles but continue to ensure that the body remains tight and straight (fig. 56). When balance appears to be stable the coach can release the grip for a few seconds at a time. When ready to come down, the gymnast should land with one foot at a time.

The supported handstand will need to be practised many times before the gymnast is able to perform the move well without support. It can also be practised against other supports such as wall-bars, but care must then be taken

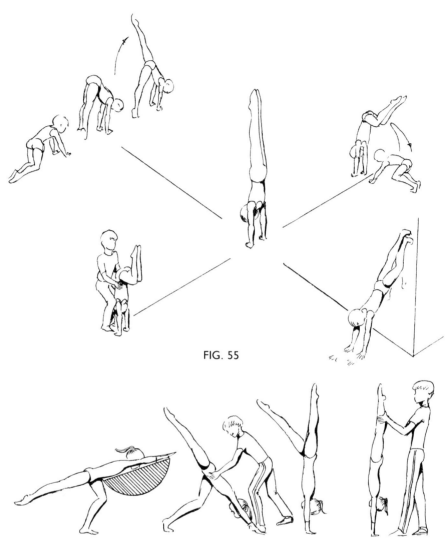

FIG. 55

FIG. 56

not to encourage a weak handstand position, with the gymnast bending over towards the support.

Faults in the handstand

1 The back is hollowed (banana shape), due to weak abdominals.

2 Lack of balance, due to lack of tension in the body.

3 Inability to get fully up to handstand, due to a push being made with the heel of the hand instead of the weight being taken on the whole of the flat hand.

4 If the shoulders are stiff, the gymnast cannot bring them over the arms and cannot lift them to the balance position. (When vaulting and performing the handspring, it is necessary to drop, then extend the shoulders to give flight and push from the hands.)

■ HANDSTAND FORWARD ROLL

When the gymnast can hold a strong handstand unsupported, they can progress to a handstand forward roll. This is a better method of getting out of the handstand than taking the legs over to bridge.

The handstand should be held in balance for a second. Then, as balance begins to be lost forwards, the head is tucked in, with the chin to the chest so that the neck and shoulders, not the head, roll on to the mat. It may be easiest to teach this down a slight incline to begin with, such as a springboard.

As the shoulders touch the floor, the arms will bend, the back will round and the body goes into a forward roll to stand. A more advanced handstand forward roll is from straight arms. Here the feel of the movement is that of 'tipping' forwards out of balance and into the roll, moving from flat hands to finger-tips, then tucking in the head (fig. 57).

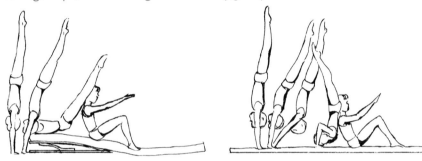

FIG. 57

(The coach can help this move by supporting the handstand balance, facing the gymnast, holding the ankles, then moving backwards, encouraging the gymnast to keep straight arms until tipped into such a position of overbalance that the gymnast must tuck in the head and roll.)

■ BACKWARD ROLL TO HANDSTAND

This is a difficult manoeuvre to achieve, requiring strength and good timing.

From a backward roll, the hips must lift high. When they are at their highest point, a strong push from the floor, a stretching of the arms and a pushing up through the shoulders lifts the body up to a handstand balance (fig. 58). Good timing is required because the body

FIG. 58

tends to either extend too soon (before the upright position is reached) or too late (the feet go straight to the floor).

■ FUN HANDSTANDS

Since the handstand is so important in gymnastics, it should be practised every day. Many ways of getting in or out of handstand should be experimented with. Variety can be added as follows.

1   Handstand against a wall or wall-bar (fig. 59a).

2   Handstand balance with different leg shapes (fig. 59b).

3   Handstand balance on one hand (fig. 59c).

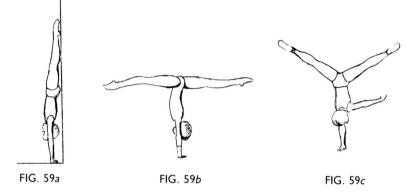

FIG. 59a   FIG. 59b   FIG. 59c

4   Walking on the hands. Stage competitions to see who can stay up the longest or who can walk the furthest.

5   Handstand, pirouette on the floor. This can be done at first with a half turn, stepping a half turn with one hand and then the other. Later the gymnast may manage a full turn or more.

6   Donkey kicks. From a strong handstand position the legs are allowed to bend over forwards, the arms slope slightly forwards and the head lifts. From this position there is a push from the hands through the shoulders, bringing the hands off the floor before the legs are piked down to land. As the gymnast lands the arms are brought up to a stretched standing position (fig. 60).

FIG. 60

7 Handstand into splits. From a strong handstand position, the legs can be lowered with control and one leg brought through the hands to a splits sitting position (fig. 61).

8 From a strong handstand, the legs can be lowered slowly in a tuck position and then the feet brought through the hands to a long sitting position (fig. 62).

FIG. 61

FIG. 62

■ *BODY ARCHES*

Many different arch shapes can be made with the body. Some are very simple, which children will enjoy making and experimenting with, and some require good body conditioning. Let the class experiment and see how many arches they can make. Try with the front to the floor, back to the floor, sideways, from head, hands, feet, shoulders or knees (fig. 63).

The bridge Most children can achieve a bridge of sorts, but to achieve a good position the gymnast must have very mobile shoulders. From back lying the hands are placed on the floor, level with the ears, with the fingers facing towards the feet. The knees are bent and the feet are flat on the floor. To reach a good shape the shoulders are pushed back, over or past the hands, legs pressed straight and together, feet flat on the floor, head between the arms. In bridge one leg and then the other can be lifted as a preliminary move to trying a back walkover. The same bridge position can be practised from sitting, preliminary to valdez (fig. 64).

Agilities

■ *HANDSPRING*

This move is a spring from the hand position on the floor. It is taken from a short run and a hurdle step, but is best learned from standing.

FIG. 63

FIG. 64

At first it may be easiest to learn from a raised platform, such as from a reuther board or from two mattresses on to one. The move is a fast handstand, one leg leading, then the other kicking up fast to join before the feet reach the floor. The body is slightly arched to come into landing with the arms stretched above the head. In the early stages the gymnast will need support from the coach.

When the gymnast can make the required shape, the handspring should be carried out from one step in. With legs together, arms just behind the body line, the gymnast takes a long, low lunge step; the arms swing up above the head and, as they reach for the mat, there is a strong leg kick from the leading leg; the arms are straight but as the legs begin to catch up with each other there is a strong push from the hands and an extension through the shoulders, giving strong propulsion from the hands. The shoulders must not push too far over the hands as they contact the floor (fig. 65).

In the initial stage, the coach should support the gymnast into a fast handstand. Stand in front of the gymnast and as the legs swing up fast and together, support the gymnast round the waist, allowing the legs to travel over your shoulder. In the next stage the coach should support under the shoulder and middle back, *guiding* the shape of the gymnast rather than lifting (fig. 66).

FIG. 65

FIG. 66

▓ *CARTWHEEL*

The start of the cartwheel can be made either forwards or sideways. It is a progression from a handstand, i.e. it is a sideways move which passes through the handstand position, but with the legs in a wide straddle position.

The cartwheel should be a rhythmic movement of hand-hand-foot-foot, as the four points touch the ground. Activities shown on pages 71-9 are among those which help the cartwheel.

1 From one side of a bench to the other. Stand, left side to the bench, place left hand on, right hand on, right leg swings over, left leg swings, crossing the bench and ending back towards the start.

2 To help the child to get the hips high, a gently sloping bench may be used. Cover the bench with a mat. The child stands far enough up it to have room to take a lunge step, placing the first hand on the bench, the second hand on the mat at the end, then the feet to the floor.

Support from the coach is from behind the gymnast, arms crossed, so that the right hand supports the left hip, the left hand the right hip, and as the gymnast performs the cartwheel, the coach's arms uncross and assist the gymnast in rotating and getting the weight fully over the shoulders (fig. 67).

Emphasise the strong push from the hands and legs in order to rotate the body and get the legs high. The move must be in a straight line; when inverted the legs should be in wide straddle. As the body comes upright the arms should still be high, close to the ears.

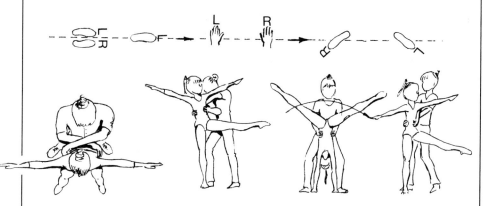

FIG. 67

■ FUN CARTWHEELS

The cartwheel lends itself to floor patterns, display work, sequences and sports acrobatics. A good cartwheel is made from a sideways starting position. Once mastered, different starting positions and other varieties can be introduced.

1 Try doing the cartwheels along a straight line on the gym floor, making sure the hand-hand-foot-foot pattern is rhythmical and accurately along the line. This is essential practice for cartwheels on bench or beam.

2 Start facing *forwards* along the line instead of sideways-on. Arms are raised, leading leg lifted then lunged straight forwards along the line. As the leading arm comes in, the body twists to the side and the side handstand is performed. The body will come up facing sideways, back to the first turn, but can then make a quarter turn forwards to complete the forward direction. This will be necessary for the cartwheel on the beam.

3 Try cartwheels in pairs – meeting each other across the gym, passing each other, meeting and returning, working facing a partner mirroring the cartwheel (fig. 68), standing very close behind a partner, moving as one, making synchronised cartwheels across the gym, or working back-to-back.

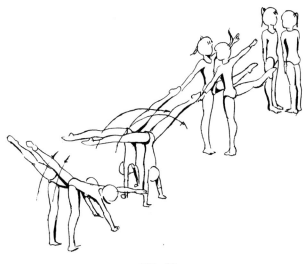

FIG. 68

4 Vary the speed of the cartwheel – very slow, wide, controlled cartwheels, or a series of very quick wheels. These are likely to be smaller than the slow ones, with not such a big step in and not such a wide split.

5 Dive cartwheels. Here two or three steps are taken into the cartwheel, the arms swing back behind the body then swing forwards into the wheel. There is momentary flight before the hands reach the mat, while the legs have already driven off the floor. Try this over an obstacle such as a rolled-up mattress.

6 One-handed cartwheel. Either the first or second hand can be used to take the weight of the cartwheel, but it is generally considered to give a better shape if the first hand is removed, making the wheel on the second hand.
   Step left to lunge into the cartwheel, take the left hand as though it were going to the mat, then swing it away to the side which will help to rotate the body. The right hand is then placed on the mat, giving a good push for the second leg (the left) which travels overhead to land, legs apart, with both hands stretched above the head (fig. 69a).

7 Vary the starting positions. The cartwheel can be made from a half kneeling position. Kneel on the right knee, left knee up and bent. The arms are stretched above the head and then the right foot gives a strong push from the ground to stretch the left leg a little and to give a slight lift from the ground. The arms now reach forwards to the ground, left then right, and the legs swing over in the cartwheel to standing (fig. 69*b*).

8 From an arabesque balance, hold the balance for a few seconds, then reach for the mat, with the raised leg leading the legs into the wheel.

9 Complete a normal cartwheel, but as the first leg lands, bend the knee and come down to half kneeling, the second leg stretched out to the side.

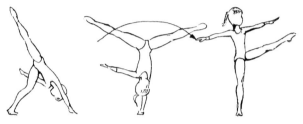

FIG. 69*a*

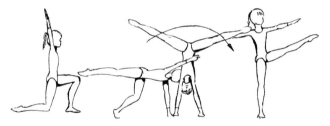

FIG. 69*b*

10 Vary the end of the cartwheel. Arrest the shape in the straddle position, hold in a straddle handstand for a second, then lower the legs to a lever-hold or straddle sit.

■ROUND-OFF OR ARAB SPRING

This is an accelerator move, usually used in conjunction with another move such as a high jump or a back flic or a somersault. Children enjoy making this move because it gives a feeling of speed and power. Coaches must beware of this since the novice gymnast can lose balance and fall backwards as the final position is off balance.

The move can be taught in isolation, from standing to begin with, and then from two or three steps entry. Similar to a cartwheel, the move finishes facing the way it began (the start of the run-in), landing with feet together. In order to achieve this there must be a turning of the hands on the floor and a hip-turn.

FIG. 70

The hand-foot pattern is shown in fig. 70. A long step is taken with the second foot and a long reach made with the second hand. There is a powerful push from the hands to bring the legs over the top of the body. The body should be stretched and the shoulder angle open.

The legs join in the air just beyond the vertical and snap down strongly to land with feet together. The strong push from the hands also helps the body to stretch strongly upwards. There is a time when the body is free in the air, with the upper body rising and the feet driving down.

▥ BACK FLIC

At first this is taught from standing but since it will normally come from a cartwheel or a round-off, it must be remembered that it will be coming from an off-balance position.

To start learning the flic, the gymnast stands with arms stretched above the head. It is as well to have two coaches supporting at first, as children find going backwards daunting. This move should only be taught to the advanced school gymnast and only if the coaches are truly familiar with the move and its support.

The gymnast flexes forwards at the hips, tending to fall backwards, with the coaches supporting with one hand behind the lower neck and one in the small of the back. At first the gymnast does not attempt to turn over, but only to jump back so that the weight is taken by the coaches.

The next stage is taken by the coaches kneeling down, one hand in the small of the back and one behind the thighs to assist the drive of the legs over the head. (It is a good idea to have the gymnast do a back walkover first, so that the coaches can estimate the approximate shape and length of the flic to come.) When the gymnast has jumped and driven backwards and the hands reach the floor (having been free for a short time), the hands must push hard to finish the drive of the legs over, snapping the feet down, lifting the arms, with the body erect.

Vaulting

□

Landings

Before teaching vaulting it is vital to teach safe landings. These can be incorporated into warm-up, game-like activities, or specific vaulting practices.

1 Landing practices: standing jumps on the floor, with soft landings on the balls of the feet.

2 Two or three steps run, jump to land.

3 Landing from a low piece of apparatus such as a single bench, sloping bench, single box-top or low gymnastic table, backwards off wall-bar.

Mats should be provided for all but the simplest jumps to absorb the shock of landing. It is better to err on the side of caution and have two mats instead of one. For any difficult landings a mattress is essential. These may slip so it may be necessary to place a mat underneath.

Landing should be on the toes and then quickly to the balls of the feet; then to the whole foot including the heel, feet together, toes turned slightly out. (Ask the children to take up a deep squat position. They will find that the heels come off the floor and that they are in an off-balance position due to their small base. Therefore, landing with only a small knee bend improves stability).

As the gymnast comes into the jump the arms should swing behind the body line and then swing forwards and upwards to increase the height of the jump (fig. 71). The arms should remain up until the jump and landing are complete.

FIG. 71

Flight

In order to make a good landing there must first be good upward flight from the apparatus, with the body stretched in the air before landing. A slight bend of the hips, knees and ankles precedes the upward jump and the body should not be hollowed during this upward flight; if anything the body should be slightly piked at the hips, with the arms stretched well above the head during flight. As the body comes in to land, the legs reach forwards to the floor with some pike in the hips and bending at the knees and ankles.

Take-off

After learning landings and flight, the gymnast needs to master the take-off. Again, this can be included in warm-up games and practices.

Take-off can be from one foot (single) or from two feet (double); the latter is the more usual for vaulting. The single take-off is from one foot to one foot, as in a jump over a puddle or a leap over an obstacle. The double take-off is from two feet to two feet and is preceded by a hurdle step when the run is converted by an approach step into a double beat, often taken in vaulting from a springboard or trampette.

Games and practices for landings, flight and take-off

Since a good run is essential for effective vaulting, all running practices can be useful.

1 Running with speed changes, at first slow and then to maximum acceleration. Good spacing and controlled direction changes are vital here.

2 Alternate running, with bouncing on the spot, gives the gymnast the feel of the difference between forward and upward movement.

3 Running and leaping, one foot to one foot, over mats or chalk marks.

4 Place mats, hoops, balls, benches or other small obstacles around the gym floor and have the class jumping, one foot to one foot, one foot to two feet, two feet to one, two to two.

5 Small groups of three or four play 'Follow my leader' over the apparatus, varying the take-off and landing.

6 Measuring the upward jump. Gymnasts in two's or three's. Stand one gymnast side-on to a wall and, with arms high above the head, chalk his/her top finger mark on the wall. With arms above the head, the gymnast performs a standing upward jump and the new height is recorded. Finally, the same measuring is recorded, but the gymnast swings the arms forwards and upwards as the jump is performed. There should be about a 5cm improvement.

■ LANDING PRACTICES

I Using low platform apparatus the gymnast steps on to the apparatus and then from a high, stretched upward jump, lands with arms stretched and a slight bend in the hips, knees and ankles.

2 Vary landing practice by jumping off with different shapes. Stretched jumps, straddle, pike, star, half turning, tuck, are all shapes which can be used (fig. 72).

FIG. 72

3 Variety in shape can also be made by encouraging gymnasts to think in terms of symmetry and asymmetry. Jumps off apparatus can be made showing symmetrical arm shapes – both arms in 'Y' shape, in star, low 'V' shape and others which the gymnasts can devise.

4 The same variety can be made with changes in leg symmetry, or asymmetric shapes can be used with either arms or legs being changed (fig. 73).

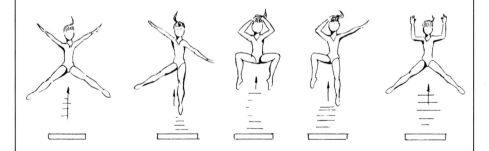

FIG. 73

5 Children can have fun with these shapes, following each other with the same shape, facing a partner, mirroring them or trying to make the opposite pattern.

▧ WEIGHT ON THE HANDS
Almost all vaults have the weight supported on both hands; in fact, in girls' competition the vault is not valid unless it is performed from both hands. In some advanced men's vaulting, one-armed vaults are acceptable, indeed highly tariffed.

It is therefore important to practise positions where the weight is over the hands.

I Put both hands on the floor and find ways of moving round them – clockwise, anti-clockwise, running, skipping, hopping, etc (fig. 74).

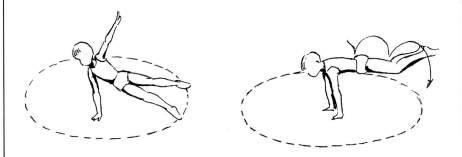

FIG. 74

2 Crouch jumps on the floor. The weight is jumped on to the hands, head held back, hands well forwards on outstretched arms, hips high and knees bent, feet together. (Various crouch jumps are also described on pages 71–2 all these are useful in vault practice.)

3 Cat spring on the floor. This is similar to a crouch jump in the sense that the jump is made on to outstretched hands, but instead of the legs bending, they are stretched and straddled behind the body. Cat springs can be made on the spot or moving round the room.

▧ HURDLE STEP
Before these jumps can be turned into vaults, a run into a take-off must be mastered; children often find this difficult. From two or three steps run, the last step is a hurdle step into a double take-off – this is from one foot to two feet. It may be easier to teach by taking two or three steps along a bench and then leaving the end of the bench from one foot, landing on a mat or springboard on two feet and jumping upwards (fig. 75).

Another relevant practice is to take a short run into a single take-off over a large ball, landing on two feet to rebound into the double take-off (fig. 76).

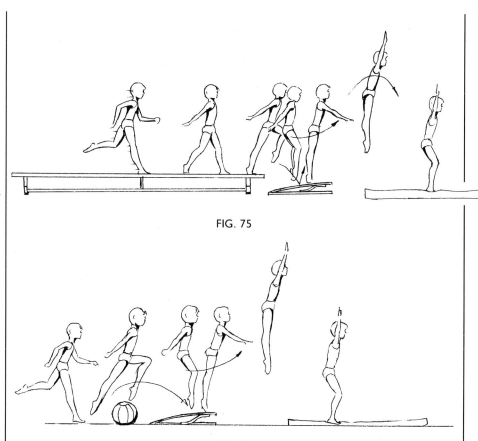

FIG. 75

FIG. 76

The vaults

■ *CROUCH VAULT OR BUNNY JUMP*

This is the safest and easiest vault to learn. At its early stage it can be practised on the floor, on, over, up and along a bench. When practised on to apparatus the vault is in two phases – hips high to achieve a jump on to the apparatus and then high again to leave the vault. This is an important vault because it encourages the weight-over-the-hands position, essential for all good vaulting. The gymnast must be taught to place the hands opposite each other and to cross the apparatus sideways, with a good grip on its sides. If they are not turned outwards, with both hands to the side, then the legs will cross the apparatus in a forward position and the child may trip or may remove one hand and distort the vault.

Children should be encouraged to experiment with the crouch vault as it can be adapted to suit all abilities. Many different pieces of apparatus can be used – a partner's back, bench, low box, bar or Swedish beam, gymnastic table, sloping bench, two benches on top of each other, horse, bar box or even a rope held by two partners (fig. 77).

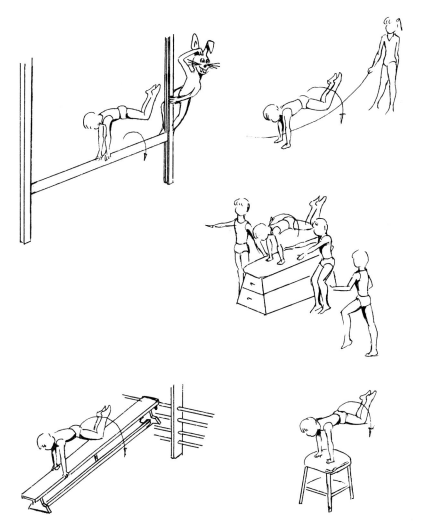

FIG. 77

▨ STRADDLE-TYPE VAULTS: LEAPFROG AND CAT SPRING

These are progressions on the crouch jump which some gymnasts find easy but others hesitate to perform because, unlike crouch where the hands remain safely in contact until the vault is performed, in straddle vaults the hands must be removed early in order to allow the body to pass over the apparatus.

There are many practices which can familiarise the gymnast with the vault before attempting the full straddle vault, such as leapfrog and cat spring vaults.

Warm-up jumps as preparation for vault

I Straddle jumps on the spot.

2 Two or three steps run followed by a straddle jump.

3 Step on to low apparatus, then high straddle jump-off.

4   Small apparatus scattered over the floor, such as large balls, skittles, ropes, mats. Children run and straddle jump over each (fig. 78).

5   Using a partner bent over as for leapfrogs or low apparatus, the gymnast puts hands on partner's back or apparatus and, pushing on it, practises straddle jumps upwards but does not attempt to jump on to or over the support (fig. 79).

6   A partner assists an upward straddle jump by facing the jumper with lower arms held out in front of the body and the gymnast's lower arms on top, supporting an upward jump (fig. 80). This is best done with a small jump followed by a high straddle jump.

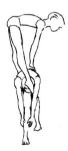

FIG. 78

FIG. 79   FIG. 80

7 Cat spring jump along the floor, springing on to the hands, legs straight and straddled behind (fig. 81).

8 Moving along the top of a bench, cat spring over an obstacle such as a large ball. From a crouch position, spring on to the hands on the far side of the ball, legs lifted, straight and straddled behind, then coming round the sides of the ball, to land beyond it (fig. 82).

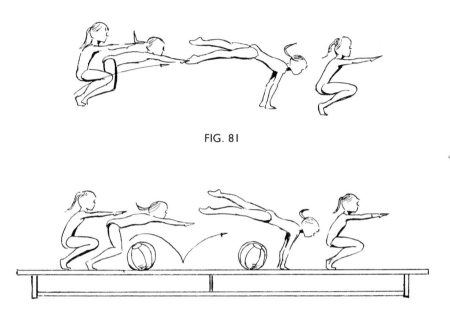

FIG. 81

FIG. 82

Leapfrog and leapfrog games

Leapfrog over a partner's back is the early stage of training for the straddle vault. The partner should make the back sideways-on to the gymnast, head well tucked in, with a mat for landing. (The jump should not be made with the support's seat towards the vaulter because if the jump lands short it will be on the neck of the support.)

This is an excellent vault to teach in three's because the third gymnast begins to learn support techniques. They should stand close to the 'back', facing the vaulter, and as the gymnast starts the vault, lean forwards to support. As the vaulter crosses the back the catcher grasps both arms firmly above the elbows and moves back with the gymnast, being careful not to impede the straddled legs.

Leapfrog is a useful vault to teach because it can be performed with suitable height variation to suit the child, though in the first attempts it is advisable to match children for size and ability. Most gymnasts will soon learn to vault alone and can then move on to variations and to cat spring and straddle vaults.

1 Leapfrog over a partner. Gymnast takes two or three steps, hurdles into a double beat and then leapfrogs over back.

2 With a line of four or five backs, well spaced, the gymnast leapfrogs the first, takes one or two steps and over the second to the end of the line, making a back, and the line moves down one place.

3 With a line of four or five backs, close together, the gymnast jumps the first and the landing from that jump acts as the double take-off for the next jump and so on down the line.

4 Leapfrog over two backs standing close together. Two gymnasts stand close together (head-to-tail makes a more compact shape); the vaulter runs, double beat, hands on the further back, and leapfrogs the double back.

5 Circle race – double circle with each of inside circle sitting in front of partner. On 'Go', inside circle crawls through partners' legs; all run clockwise round the circle until they reach their partner again, when they leapfrog over them and sit.

■ CAT SPRING VAULT

This can be performed on a box, bar box or horse (with no handles), or gymnastic table, all placed lengthways, or from the end of two benches placed on top of each other. Mats should be provided for landing.

From a crouch position on the top of the apparatus, the gymnast springs forwards on to the hands, in the cat spring shape, arms straight, head lifted, legs high, stretched and straddled. Then the gymnast pushes off with the hands to let body and legs cross over the end of the apparatus to a steady landing, feet together well beyond the end of the apparatus.

At first, using a long piece of apparatus such as a box, the gymnast will need to crouch jump on to the end of the apparatus, make a small jump along the top and then cat spring off the far end. Eventually the better gymnasts will be able to perform the full vault.

In the full vault, the first crouch jump takes the gymnast well along the top of the apparatus (the hands must reach well forwards on take-off to achieve this) and then they will be far enough along the top of the apparatus to cat spring straight off. The cat spring should show good body lift, weight on outstretched hands, body straight, legs stretched and feet about level with the box-top as the straddle takes place along the top. Thrust from the hands pushes the upper body away from the apparatus so that a stretched position can be achieved before landing (fig. 83). Good vaulting should always show clear flight, with the body stretched and the landing well away from the apparatus.

■ STRADDLE VAULT

After leapfrog over backs or low apparatus and cat spring off apparatus have been mastered, the gymnast can move on to straddle vault.

This can be performed most easily over a vaulting buck because it is not as wide as a box or horse. Beam saddles or a low vaulting table may also be used. Using a box or horse, with or without handles, the apparatus is placed widthways. These must be at a suitable height for the age, size and ability of the gymnast, but the higher apparatus will certainly need a springboard or reuther board. (Do not have the apparatus too high for the gymnast; many children have been put off vaulting for ever by the sight of an enormous horse rearing in front of them.)

From a good, fast, dynamic run, the arms swing back, the gymnast hurdles into a double take-off, and the arms swing forwards on to the middle of the apparatus, shoulder width apart. Then the legs lift and straddle across the vault and with a strong thrust from the arms, the body lifts to allow the legs through and the body to stretch before landing (fig. 84). A more advanced straddle will show a stretched flight, prior to take-off.

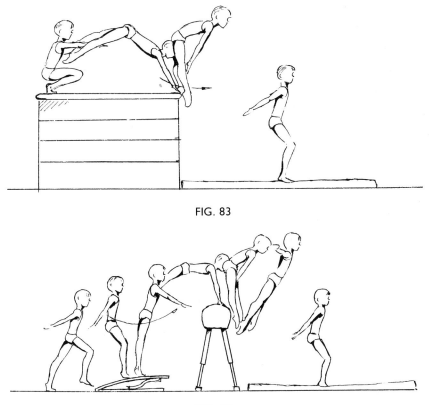

FIG. 83

FIG. 84

LONG ASTRIDE VAULT OR LONG FLY

The best gymnasts will manage a straddle vault over the long box, but a springboard or reuther board is important here. This can be practised best over a buck, lengthways, to begin. When first starting the vault over a long box, try getting the crouch vault on to the box, well along the top with the feet. This will be done with a strong take-off and swinging the arms so that the hands reach well to the far end of the apparatus (fig. 85). When this can be performed well the gymnast can attempt the full straddle over the length of the box, with the coach either facing the box and grasping both upper arms as the gymnast reaches the end, moving backwards as the gymnast leaves the box, or at the side, grasping the nearest upper arm and moving forwards with the gymnast, keeping out of the way of the straddled legs.

FIG. 85

▨ FORWARD ROLL ON TO APPARATUS

Strictly speaking, the forward roll is not a vault but is useful for take-off practice and as a progression for headspring, and can lead to various dismounts.

After a good forward roll has been learnt on the floor, it can be transferred to other apparatus. Using the box lengthways, three forward rolls can be taught.

1 Crouch jump on to the end of the long box, lie along the top, lower the hands down to the mats at the far end and roll off the end of the box (fig. 86a).

2 Crouch jump on to the end of the box, forward roll along the top of the box to stand and high jump-off (fig. 86b).

3 From a double beat take-off, grip the box at each side and with hips high and head tucked in, forward roll along the box-top to standing and show a variety of jumps off (fig. 86c).

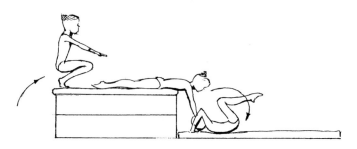

FIG. 86a

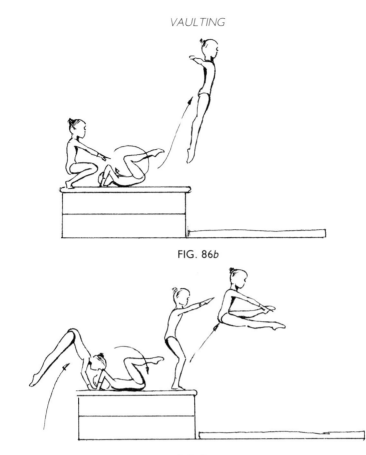

FIG. 86*b*

FIG. 86*c*

Dismounts

1 Various dismount jumps can be added to rolls along the box – high upward jumps with tuck, pike, straddle, turning jumps and symmetric and asymmetric shapes.

2 The box can be extended by another piece of apparatus, with a mattress on top, so that additional rolls can take place down a bench or springboard (fig. 87).

3 The dismount can be to the side of the apparatus, a jump off sideways, half turn on the top, or crouch jump off to the side (fig. 88).

The gymnasts can probably work out many more dismounts.

FIG. 87

FIG. 88

HEADSPRING

A good headspring must first be taught on the floor before it can be transferred to apparatus.

I To get the feel of using a box for headspring in the early stage of the vault, the gymnast can perform the headspring along the top of the long box from a crouch position at the end (fig. 89).

2 The second stage is to perform the vault from the springboard on to the near end of a low box (fig. 90).

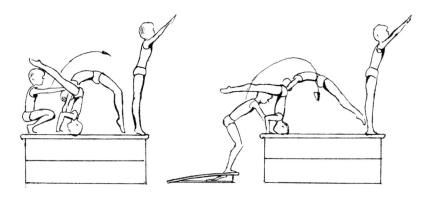

FIG. 89   FIG. 90

3 The next stage is to do the vault off the far end of the box on to a mattress or pile of mats. From a crouch position on the box-top the gymnast springs on to the hands and head and thrusts into a high arch off the box (fig. 91).
   It is important to have a spotter with this vault in its early stages. There is a long flight period when the headspring is coming from the box instead of on the floor and it is coming from a greater height. Because of this longer flight period and because the feet and hips rotate under the shoulders, there is a danger of over-rotating and falling forwards. The spotter is there therefore to prevent over-rotation and falling and also to help the gymnast maintain the high arch position. The spotter stands at the side of the box, placing the near hand under the gymnast's shoulder and the far hand under the back.

(Standing on the gymnast's right, the support has the left hand on the right shoulder and the right hand under the back.)

4 Finally, the entire vault can be performed over the broad box, horse or gymnastic table (fig. 92). From a strong take-off jump, the arms swing forwards on to the middle of the apparatus. The hips are lifted strongly above the arms, piked at the hips. Then the legs swing upwards and over with the body in an arch position. A good thrust from the hands provides an upward movement, allowing the body good flight from the apparatus and the time to straighten out before landing.

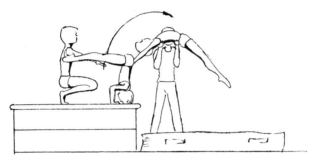

FIG. 91

FIG. 92

■ SQUAT OR THROUGH VAULTS
Many squat practices should be carried out before attempting the full vault.

1 In three's, the supports hold the gymnast by the hand and above the elbow. With two or three steps run they travel with the gymnast and then lift high for the gymnast to bend the legs up in the tuck position (fig. 93).

2 Squat jumps along the floor over an obstacle.

3 Squat jumps on a bench over an obstacle such as a large ball.

4 The squat mount can be practised on to the end of apparatus. This is a time when the feeling of a strong push from the hands and a quick release must be felt.

It is better to start with practices on to long apparatus, then the gymnast need not fear falling forwards and can get the feel of quick release of the hands. Beam saddles on the bars can also be used for this.

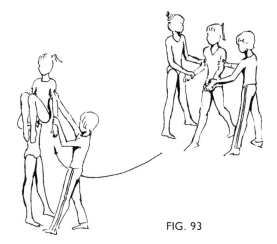

FIG. 93

Candle jump This is a preliminary vault to the squat vault. The squat is taken on to apparatus, such as the broad box, and then a strong and immediate stretch of the legs takes place into a high upward jump (fig. 94).

FIG. 94

▩ FULL SQUAT VAULT
The full squat vault can be taught on beam saddles or on the horse with handles, because the added height provided by the handles makes it easier to squat the legs through. On the other hand there is a tendency to hold on to the handles too long, spoiling the quick, strong action which is the aim of the squat vault.

When the vault is on the broad box, the arms swing forwards so that the hands are placed in the middle of the box, shoulder width apart, and the knees bend, tucking the legs through the middle of the hands. The knees must bend close to the chest and the lower legs must be kept straight, not allowed to turn to one side. This is accompanied by a strong thrust from the hands on the box-top, the chest and head are lifted and the body stretched in flight off, which should land the gymnast well in front of the box.

The run-up for the squat vault should be fast and dynamic, the take-off strong and the arms should swing fast forwards to the box (fig. 95). The legs should lift to horizontal on the first flight, but not above this as the result would be the gymnast falling forwards on landing.

At first the gymnast will need support by the coach, who should stand in at the side, grasping the gymnast with both hands above the nearer elbow and moving forwards with the vault to control the landing (fig. 96).

FIG. 95

FIG. 96

■ SQUAT OVER LONG BOX ('TIGER')

More difficult than the squat over the broad box is the same vault performed over a long box. It is essential to have a springboard here. The run must be fast, the take-off strong and the arms must swing the hands to the far end of the box. The hands must give a good push-off from the box, allowing the body to be pushing up from the box as the legs squat through and the body extends before landing (fig. 97).

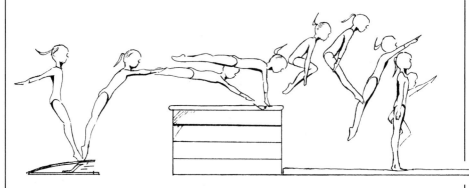

FIG. 97

■ REAR VAULT

This is an unusual vault because it comes from a single take-off, that is from one foot.

The box is placed diagonally and the gymnast approaches with a parallel diagonal run of only three or five steps. The run starts with the outside foot: thus, if the box is on the gymnast's right side, the run will be left-right-left and the right leg swings over the box; if the box is on the left, the run will be right-left-right and the left leg will swing over first.

The hand nearest the box is placed on the box-top, just before the leg swings

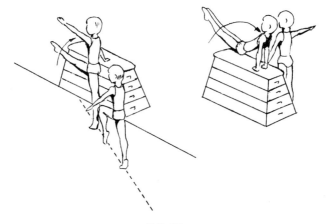

FIG. 98

over. The hand on the box-top helps to take the body weight as the nearest leg swings up and over. The second leg then swings up to join the first in a high 'V' position. The second hand joins the first on top of the box to give a strong push to enable the legs to swing up and over. The first hand releases to let the body through to land, but the second hand remains on top to steady the landing (fig. 98).

First practices for this vault can be to a sitting position on the box-top, followed by a push-off to land. When this can be accomplished the whole vault can be attempted. This vault can be made with or without a springboard.

▓ *SINGLE WOLF VAULT*

This is more easily done on a horse with handles because it allows more room for the bent legs to cross through the middle. It can also be done on a horse or box without handles.

From a double take-off, both hands on the handles, the gymnast jumps on to the top of the horse, one leg in the middle between the hands and the other leg well stretched out to the side and lifted above the top of the horse. When a clean jump can be made easily on to the top, the vault can be made right over the horse. In this case, with the left leg in the middle and the right leg stretched to the side, the right hand must be released quickly to allow the body to pass over the horse. The vault should be practised to the left and right sides.

▓ *DOUBLE WOLF*

The wolf vault can be performed with both legs crossing on the same side of the handles. The legs must be straight and together and lifted high enough to be parallel to the horse-top, with the body facing forwards. Again, the hand on the leg side must be released quickly to let the body over.

▓ *HANDSTAND-OFF OR WATERFALL*

This is an early preparation for the handspring vault. A good handstand must first be taught on the floor before being attempted from the box. The gymnast makes a squat on to the top of the box and then moves towards the landing end. Then he/she takes a lunge step into a handstand position, holds it straight and then with a slight push from the hands allows the feet to travel over the head to land feet first on the mat.

There is some danger here of over-rotation so it is essential that a coach stands in support with this vault. The coach stands at the end of the box and supports the gymnast in the handstand position with the nearest hand under the gymnast's shoulder and the second hand supporting the back as the body arches over. The coach should not release until the gymnast has landed safely.

▓ *HANDSPRING VAULT*

This is the lowest tariffed of the vaults recognised by the FIG. Nevertheless, it is a very important vault because it forms the basis of many of the more advanced vaults. It is vital that it is performed well since more difficult vaults cannot be tackled until the handspring has been mastered correctly. Previously called 'The long arm', it is an overthrow vault in the handstand position.

The vault demands good body tension. This can be trained by getting the gymnast to perform a very good, straight handstand and then starting to train this as a vault. To begin with it is advisable to teach the vault from a low box-top on to a pile of mattresses which is at least level with the box-top. First, kick up to handstand on the top and then fall flat on to the mattresses. The landing must be quite flat with heels, bottom and shoulders all landing together (fig. 99a). Then the box and mattresses can all be raised higher and the vault taken from a short, fast run.

When this can be performed with good body tension, the pile of mattresses can be removed and the true vault started. It will need good support for some time. Some coaches like to stand in to support, on the take-off side of the box or horse between the springboard and the apparatus, to help lift the gymnast over. With the school vaulter, it is recommended to have also support on the landing side, on the gymnast's other side.

There should be no pike position shown in the body as the flight on is made; in fact, the top vaulters will show a very slight dish or hollow. Repulsion from the top of the apparatus should be fast with a strong thrusting action through the arms and shoulders and the gymnast should not remain in contact with the apparatus beyond the vertical position.

The second flight should take the gymnast well away from the apparatus, giving time and height for the body to stretch into landing (fig. 99b).

FIG. 99a

FIG. 99b

Fun vaults

Only when vaults such as squat and straddle can be performed safely (and then only with the more confident and proficient gymnasts), can unsupported fun and display vaulting take place.

1   Vaulting in stream. When simple vaults can be executed safely, taking the normal time between gymnasts, vaulting can be speeded up so that as one gymnast takes off, the next one starts the run; there then becomes a continuous stream of gymnasts over the apparatus.

This can be an effective display item but care must be taken to provide adequate landing area and to teach the gymnasts how to roll out of the way if they fall on landing. The vault must not be allowed to continue for too long because it is very tiring and will become dangerous as the gymnasts slow up.

2   For display purposes it is possible to use the apparatus in more than one direction. For example, one line of gymnasts may straddle vault over the broad box with alternate gymnasts cat-springing on the long box (fig. 100*a*).

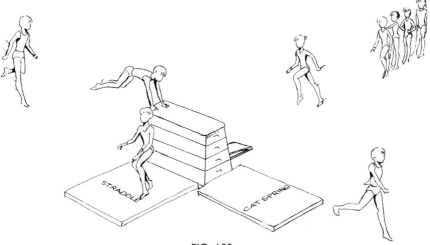

FIG. 100*a*

3   Apparatus may build up so that a series of vaults takes place, linked by other moves in a sequence. For example: cat spring on to a long box, off on to a set of mats, two cartwheels, three steps run, leapfrog a vaulting buck (fig. 100*b*). Or: crouch jumps up a sloping bench on to a bar box, forward roll along the box-top, high jump-off, forward roll, handstand forward roll, crouch jump over a bar.

4   The very competent gymnast may be able to vault more than one piece of apparatus; for example, a buck placed widthways in front of a box which is lengthways. (In fact, this is a good practice for getting gymnasts to get their legs high on take-off by making them get over the buck in order to get their feet on to the box.)

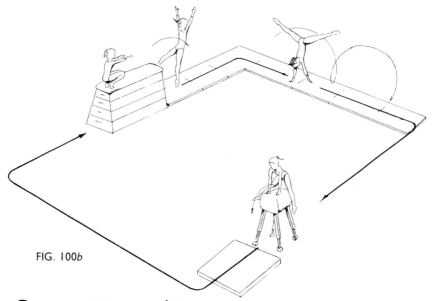

FIG. 100*b*

Competitive vaulting

Vaults which are performed in national or international competitions are listed by the FIG (the Federation Internationale Gymnastique) and given a tariff value according to their difficulty.

In girls' competition the simplest vault tariffed is the handspring. This is given 8.50, which means that even if the vault is perfect, only 8.50 can be scored. The same vault in the boys' code is tariffed at 8.60. For girls the most difficult vaults are scored out of 10.00 and these are mainly vaults with turns and somersaults added to basic vaults, such as handsprings with two full turns, handsprings with front somersaults and vaults with backward take-off from round-offs. Boys are scored up to 9.80 and can receive a bonus of 0.2 for extremely high and long vaults.

But many of the vaults described in the previous pages may be used in junior codes or school competitions and are vaults used in the Award schemes. Squat and straddle vaults are frequently used in British school competitions, as is handspring, and in these circumstances vaults which land on apparatus and then show flight off, such as candle jump or cat spring, will usually be marked from a lower total. In British school competitions, long fly, headspring, squat-on and straddle-jump-off, are all recognised as competition vaults.

In women's vaulting, competitors are permitted two attempts at a vault and the higher mark counts. In fact, they may change their vault and attempt a different vault for their second choice. In men's vault, only one attempt is permitted.

In most school competitions, boys and girls are both allowed two vaults each and these may be the same or different, but each competition may devise its own rules and, while there is a set height and apparatus size for FIG competitions, school events may vary dimensions to suit the size, age and ability of the children.

Skills and activities using apparatus

□

Benches

The gymnastic bench is one of the most versatile pieces of equipment in the gymnasium. It can be used broad side up, narrow side up, on its side, hooked on to a wall-bar, bar box, ladder or A-frame. It can be used as a bridge between apparatus, covered with a mat to give a soft practice area, employed as a take-off board or used for balance.

▓ *FITNESS OR CIRCUIT TRAINING*

1 Stand on the broad side of a bench, jump feet astride to the floor and rebound back on to the bench again. Keep this up for a specified length of time or for a certain number of jumps.

2 Stand on the floor facing the bench, step up with right foot, join left foot on bench-top, step down, left, join right. Repeat, starting with left foot.

3 With feet together, facing the bench, jump both feet on to bench and off backwards to the starting side.

4 Feet together, side to the bench, continuous jumps on to bench and off the opposite side.

5 Feet together, side to the bench, continuous jumping side to side, passing right over the bench each time.

All these are good cardio-vascular exercises and may form part of a circuit training course. They are also strong leg strengthening exercises.

▓ *JUMPS*

1 For the youngest children, bunny jumps along the top of the broad surface of the bench are a good starting exercise for later jumps and vaults. The hands should grip the sides of the bench and move along a step with each jump. The children should be encouraged to get their seats as high as possible with each jump, weight over the hands.

2 Bunny jumps from the top of the bench to the left side, then back on, then to the right side and back on.

3 Single bench, broad side up, bunny jumps from side to side, crossing right over the bench each time. The children should grip the bench each side and try to get the seat high (fig. 101a). Older children may be able to do this with two benches placed one on top of the other, but this is not very stable and a child should sit on each end of the benches to steady them.

4 As above, but made more difficult, to suit the size and age of the child, by sloping the bench hooked on to wall-bars, ladders, an A-frame or bar box (fig. 101b).

5 More advanced still is with the bench sloping as above, but the gymnast starts at the top and crouch jumps from side to side, travelling down the bench from top to bottom. This is more difficult since the gymnast is wary of having the seat far above the head, but is a useful exercise because the child can start as far up or down the bench as ability will allow.

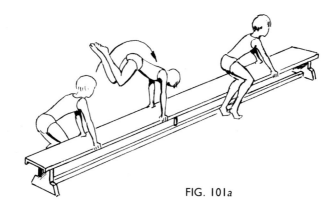

FIG. 101a

FIG. 101b

▩ *LANDING PRACTICE*

Before vaulting can be taught, the gymnast must be instructed in how to land safely and here the benches can be used in many ways.

1 At first a simple step on to the bench, jump in the air and land on the balls of the feet with a slight give in the ankles and a bend of the knees.

2 Then a sloping bench can be added to give extra height. With a bench fixed to wall-bars, the child runs up the bench and jumps off at the top, jumping to the side.

3 The sloping bench can be fixed to much of the primary school apparatus, such as tables or A-frames, where the child can run up to the top, step on the top of the table and jump off on to mats. After a good landing has been achieved from a straight jump, all the other varieties of jump shape can be introduced.

4 The bench can also be useful in teaching single and double take-offs: a running jump with a take-off from one foot to the other can be made round the room over benches and then the same can be done with a double take-off.

▩ *ROLLS*

Most children can learn to roll forwards quickly but find the backward roll more difficult. It may help to teach this by having them back roll down a gentle slope such as a springboard covered with a mat.

1 Forward roll along the top of a broad bench covered by a thin mat (fig. 102a).

2 Backward roll along a bench-top (fig. 102b).

3 Forward roll from the bench-top off the end and on to a mat.

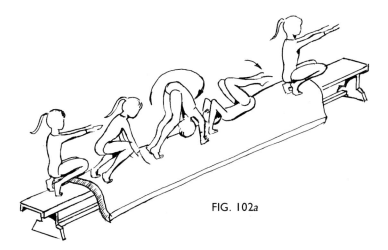

FIG. 102a

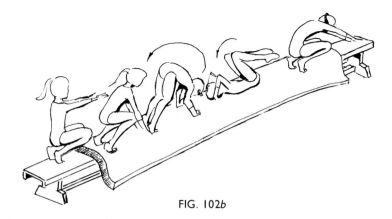

FIG. 102*b*

4   Roll over a bench from one side to the other, with a mattress as a landing area (fig. 103).

5   Two benches close together side by side and covered with a mat, gently sloping from a bar: forward or backward rolls down the benches (fig. 104).

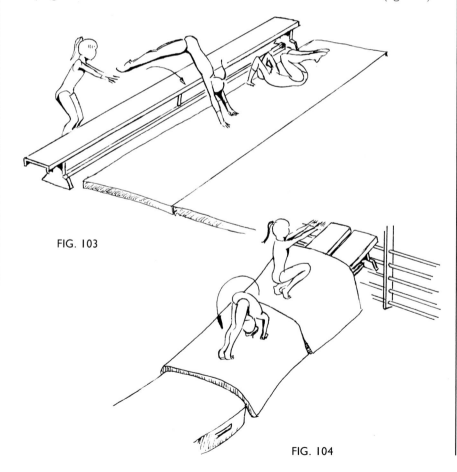

FIG. 103

FIG. 104

■ CARTWHEEL PRACTICES

1   Early teaching of cartwheels can consist of getting the child standing at the side of a bench, hands as for bunny jump but crossing from one side of the bench to the other, and lifting the legs straight, with a half turn to land (fig. 105).

2   Another cartwheel practice is with one foot on the ground at the end of a bench, taking the hands then the leading foot into a cartwheel shape along the bench-top, the body half-turning as the second foot comes on to the bench (fig. 106).

3   Cartwheels from the end of a bench off on to a mat.

4   When the gymnast is proficient at cartwheels, they can be performed along the top of a bench. This is valuable practice for the advanced move of the cartwheel on the balance beam (fig. 107). (As a preparation for this the gymnast can perform cartwheels along any line on the gym floor.)

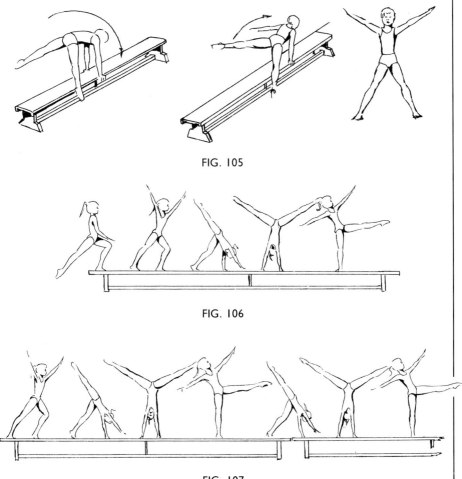

FIG. 105

FIG. 106

FIG. 107

■BALANCES

To begin with, all balances should be learned and practised along the broad side of the bench but as the gymnast becomes more proficient, some can be transferred to the narrow side of the turned-over bench.

1   Walking with good posture along the bench, head up, body erect, stomach and seat tucked in, feet well stretched.

2   Skipping along the bench, good footwork, well on the toes.

3   Many different jumps and steps can be introduced along the bench-top – split jump, cat jump, hopping, dance steps such as chassé, komat, and spins and turns.

4   Held balances on one leg can show great variety and the child can be very creative (fig. 108). The arabesque balance can exhibit several varieties – bent front leg, straight leg, back leg bent or straight, arms in opposition or same arm as leg.

FIG. 108

5   Balances may be on parts of the body other than the feet. Those on the seat, knee, shoulder and head can all look effective and be fun to experiment with. They can form a basis for more advanced work later on. Practise them on the floor first (fig. 109).

6   Some balances can be performed part on the bench and part on the floor. The handstand and headstand can both be executed on the floor beside a bench, with one hand on the floor and one on the bench (fig. 110).

7   Handstand balances can be performed on the bench. At first it is advisable to make the handstand and then come down to land astride the bench. Later these balances can come down to the broad surface but a mat should be placed on at first.

8   Various shapes of handstand can be used – stag, split, straddle.

9   Handstand forward roll can be taught to the best gymnasts, but a mat should certainly be placed on the bench (fig. 111).

10   With a mat close beside the bench, the gymnast can do a high shoulder roll and then, with a quarter turn towards the bench, bring the seat quickly to the bench and sit up on it. (This must be performed with the body close to the bench.)

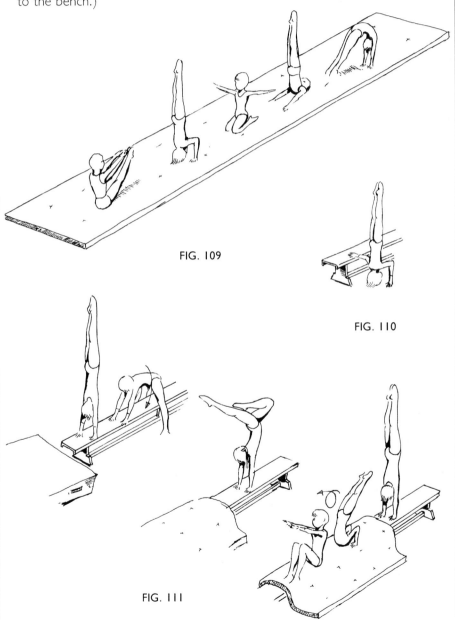

FIG. 109

FIG. 110

FIG. 111

■ PULLING AND SLIDING MOVEMENTS

I   Small children enjoy sliding close to the floor and can pull themselves along the floor, winding in and out underneath the bench.

2   Seal glide along the bench-top. The gymnast holds the bench firmly at each side and pulls along the top on the stomach, pulling between the arms. The child should be encouraged to reach well forwards with the arms and again as the body is pulled through to show good extension of body, legs and feet (fig. 112).

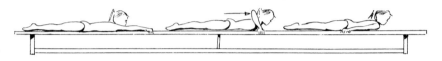

FIG. 112

3   The strength of this move can be increased by making the pull up an inclined bench.

4   Lying on the back and reaching back behind the head, the seal glide can also be performed on the back.

■ BENCHES AS BRIDGES OR PLATFORMS

Interesting areas can be made by combining benches with bars. Two or three benches can be hooked on to the bars with their other end on top of a box. The box is jammed up against the benches so that they are against the end of the lower rung and cannot slip. The benches, now with surfaces close

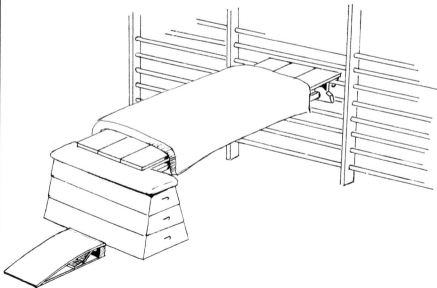

FIG. 113

together, form a wide platform which, covered by mats, makes a bridge across which moves such as rolls and cartwheels can be performed.

This apparatus can then be used in many ways to facilitate a series of movements such as: run, jump from a board on to the box, cartwheel across the bench bridge and climb up the frame at the far side. This can also be constructed with the mats on a slight slope, assisting rolls forwards or backwards down the slope (fig. 113).

Ropes

Ropes in school gyms may be found in sets which pull out from the wall on a pulley system, as part of the Southampton Cave system, as part of junior school frame systems where they may hang freely and can be used for swinging, or may be fixed to the frame top and bottom. In some gyms they may be spaced and positioned in such a way that they can be used in conjunction with Swedish beams, in which case exciting combinations of apparatus can be devised.

1 Small children all enjoy swinging on a rope and will quickly learn to hang on with hands and feet and swing.

2 Swinging on double ropes, arms bent and held at head height, body straight, is a good early training for ring work.

3 Swing on two ropes, bring the legs high on the forward swing, arching the body, and jump off forwards (fig. 114).

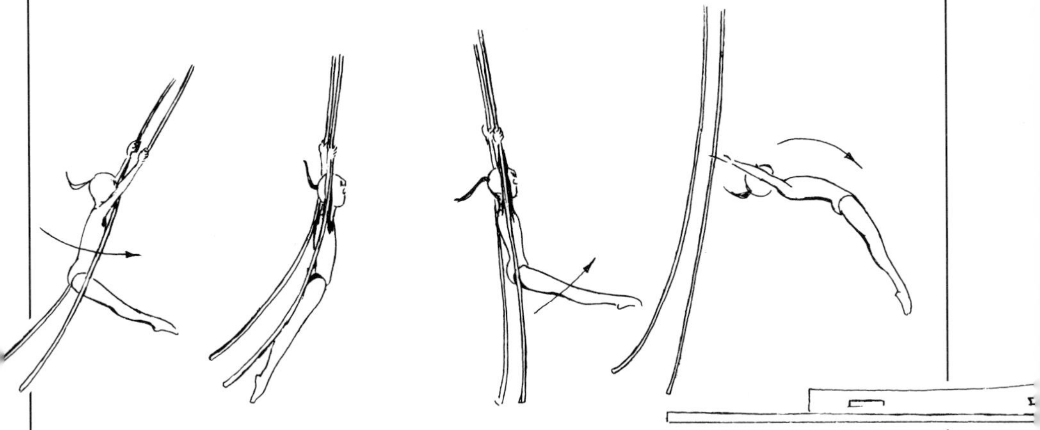

FIG. 114

4 Monkey hang. Hanging upside down on a single rope, stretching the legs well up the rope with the end hanging down like a tail.

5 Swallow hang. This is performed on two ropes. Holding at head height, the legs swing up and back between the ropes, then the feet hook on to one rope each and the body is hollowed, head raised and looking towards the way the gymnast faced to begin (fig. 115).

6 Back and forward turnover between two ropes. Holding between two ropes at head height, the legs tuck up, the head drops back, and the feet and legs are rolled back over the head to land behind the head and ropes. The arms are then still holding on above the body and the hands must not let go but hold on as the feet bounce on the floor and the body rolls forwards again between the arms, to stand (fig. 116).

FIG. 115

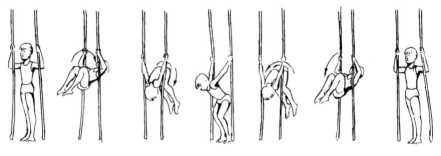

FIG. 116

7 Rope climbing. The rope should be gripped between the ankles, running over the lower ankle and held tightly between the top heel and the lower ankle. The hands should move hand-over-hand up the rope. The correct rhythm is: hands 1-2-3, pull up the legs, hands 1-2-3, pull up the legs. Each time the legs are pulled up they should be released and change, left leg over right, right over left. This is difficult to achieve, particularly on ropes which get very slippery, but what is important is that the child is taught to come down hand-over-hand and not slide down, since very nasty rope burns can result. Where ropes are knotted at intervals, the child will find it much easier to get a grip and learn to climb.

8 Very strong exercise is given by the gymnast climbing up and down ropes without holding on with the legs. Even stronger is to hold the legs straight out in front as climbing takes place.

9 Where there are several ropes in a line, diagonal climbing involves moving upwards and across from rope to rope to finish at the top of the last rope. Starting up the first rope, the climber goes up a short distance, reaches for the next rope and on bent arms hangs with a straight body between the ropes for a few seconds before transferring to the second rope (fig. 117).

FIG. 117

10 Another very strong exercise is to hang upside down, as in monkey hang, and then climb upside down hand-over-hand.

11 Standing on apparatus, hold well up the rope and swing off.

12 This can also be done holding between two ropes.

13 Where ropes will reach to a pull-out bar, it is fun to stand on the bar and swing off, then try to swing back to stand on the bar again.

14 Very exciting for confident gymnasts is to have a row of children standing on a Swedish beam holding a rope each. On 'Go', alternate gymnasts (1, 3, 5) swing off and as they swing back, 2, 4, 6 swing off. It is necessary that *alternate* gymnasts swing, otherwise they are too close together. It is also essential that they swing straight, that the second swing is timed exactly as the first gymnasts start their swing back, and that they go straight through the space (fig. 118).

15 Stand on a box-top and jump to catch the rope swung by a partner towards the gymnast. The rope is best taken high and dropped strongly to the jumper because if it is pushed, it tends to kink and swing short. The jumper must jump up and forwards to catch the rope high.

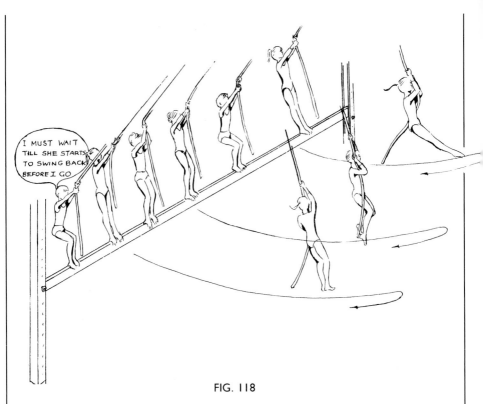

FIG. 118

16 Run along a bench, holding two ropes well up and then, as you swing forwards off the end, swing up to swallow hang.

17 Rope climbing race. This is an exciting race enjoyed by girls and boys. With six ropes, six teams are selected and sit at the base of the ropes. The first one in each team stands and on 'Go' climbs as far and as fast as possible until 'Time' is called (perhaps ten seconds). Whichever gymnast has any part of the body at the highest point scores six, then five, four, three, two, one, provided that the feet are off the ground. Individual scores add up to make a team total.

Bars and Swedish beams

Many different bars are found in schools. These are well used in most primary schools but often dusty and unused in senior schools. In many senior schools the old Swedish beams are still in the gyms and can be used for a great variety of skills. However, many teachers are unsure how to use them which is a great waste of equipment. Southampton Cave apparatus is still found in many schools and, with all its different attachments, can provide many opportunities for skill training which is valuable for later, more advanced work on bars and rings. Wall-bars, too, and many of the frame-type apparatus found in primary schools can be used in an imaginative way to suit all types of gymnast. Some of the primary school apparatus includes ropes, ladders and climbing frames within the structure, and benches and ladders which can be hooked on to add to the activities to be explored.

◼ *SWEDISH BEAMS*

Swedish beams have an upright which has to be pulled out from the wall and fixed into the floor; then single or double beams pull down and are pegged in at the required height. Often, what is not realised is that they can be pushed right down to the ground, turned over and made into a balance beam, though they may wobble somewhat and require the support of a wooden wedge.

Such beams are of great value for strength and circuit training. They can be used for vaulting, in combination with ropes and as a starter for most later work required on bars and rings.

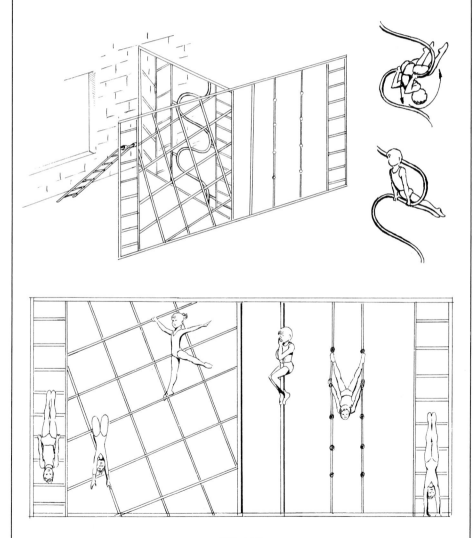

FIG. 119

Two main grips are used on bars or Swedish beams – overgrasp or under-grasp. For backward and upward circles from the ground on the Swedish beam, undergrasp is required. On a round bar, such as found in Southampton Cave or in an attachment to frames, overgrasp will be used. In undergrasp on a wide bar the thumb and fingers are forwards and under, with the bar between the body and the hands. In undergrasp on a round bar the thumbs may move quite quickly to the opposite side from the fingers, nearer the body. In overgrasp, the thumbs are held forwards with the fingers.

■ WARM-UP ACTIVITIES ON BARS

Most children enjoy swinging on bars, pulling up to look over the top, trying to hook the feet on, or travelling on their hands along the bar while hanging on, body swinging. All of these can be taught as skills which when correctly performed are a basis for more advanced work.

On ladders, simply learning to climb up and down, climb up and over the top, climb up and hang away from the ladder or wall-bar with one hand and one leg released – all this will be necessary before the child gains the confidence to attempt more difficult moves.

On climbing frames, interesting shapes can be made with the body weaving in and out of squares and leading with different parts of the body.

Swinging on low bar   Swinging should be taught to make the gymnast swing the whole body, extending in front as far as possible, arms straight, hips bending as the body swings back. The shoulders must relax with the head kept between the arms (fig. 120). This is a good strengthening exercise if repeated many times and can be performed on round or Swedish beams, though these do impede the forward swing to a degree. From this swing other moves can develop.

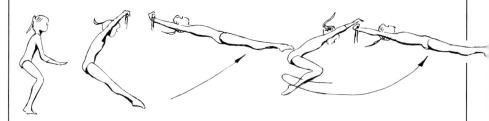

FIG. 120

Undershoot swing from floor   To do this the gymnast will need to take a step towards the bar, holding it in overgrasp, then swing the rear leg forwards and upwards as high as possible, joined quickly at the height of the swing by the second leg. The hips will follow upwards, increasing the swing, and then the body hollows as the hands are released and the feet come in to land well in front of the bar (fig. 121). This should be practised many times as it is the basis of much bar work. A good landing area should be provided.

Variations can be started from a two foot jump take-off, where the feet will be nearer the bar (fig. 122). When this has been mastered, swinging over an obstacle such as a rolled-up mattress can be introduced; this helps to increase the required arch shape. (This type of movement is also described when being performed from two ropes – *see* page 79.)

When the gymnast has achieved both a good swing and arch and is sure of a good landing, well away from the bar, a half turn can be added after release and before landing.

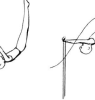

FIG. 121

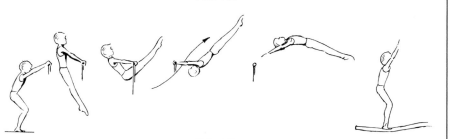

FIG. 122

Skin the cat This can be performed on any type of bar. Holding in overgrasp, the gymnast lifts both legs to between the hands to hang in half-inverted hang. Having achieved this position and held it with straight legs, they can come back to the starting position again or bend at the hips and carry on backwards to land facing the way they started having 'skinned the cat' (fig. 123).

FIG. 123

Monkey travel   Gymnasts can execute this on any type of bar and at quite a young age. Standing underneath the bar at one end, back towards the direction of travel, the hands grasp the bar above the head, one hand in front of the other, and the legs swing up and round the bar; one ankle is placed over the other, pressing the bar firmly with the back of the lower heel. The hands then move backwards along the bar, hand by hand, and the legs follow suit (fig. 124). On a slippery bar the legs may simply slide along or they may be released one at a time and step along in time with the hands.

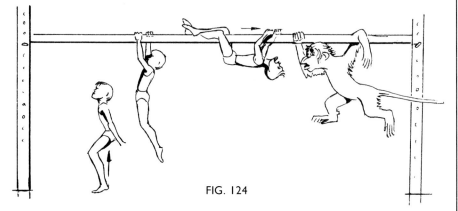

FIG. 124

Hanging like a bat   This exercise can be performed from a handstand against a bar (where the legs are allowed to drop over the top of the bar), or on a climbing frame or ladder (where the child climbs through the frame and then drops back to hang from the back of the knees). At first the hands can reach down to touch the floor but later they can be lifted from the floor and the body allowed to swing gently back and forwards (fig. 125).

Front support on bar/beam   This is a starting position for many other moves and needs to be mastered correctly before others are initiated from it.

Standing facing the bar (round or Swedish), the hands are placed on the top, shoulder width apart. With a push on the hands the gymnast jumps on to the bar with the body resting against the bar (which runs across the top of the thighs, **not** against the groin). The arms should be straight, shoulder width apart, legs and feet together, body sloping at an angle against the bar (fig. 126). On a Swedish beam the thumbs should be turned

FIG. 125

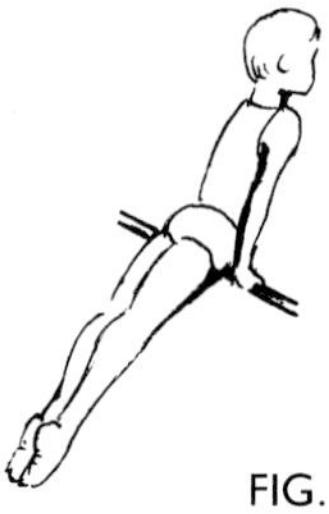

FIG. 126

forwards, fingers towards the body. The shoulders should be well down throughout the whole movement.

To dismount, the legs swing down and under the bar, piking at the hip. They then swing backwards and with a push from the hands the gymnast jumps back, well away from the beam, to land with a slight knee-bend in an upright position.

Forward hip-roll from front support to ground   From the front support position described above, a forward roll around the bar can be taught.

From front support, thumbs forwards on Swedish beam, the trunk bends forwards over the bar. When the head and shoulders have passed the horizontal, the legs pike at the hips and pass over the bar. Good control must be maintained on the bar so that the legs are lowered gently to the ground, knees bending to absorb the landing. Then the hands let go of the bar for the gymnast to stand erect on the starting side (fig. 127).

In the early attempts the coach should stand in support, holding one of the hands firmly in place on the bar and controlling the circling movement with the other hand in the small of the back.

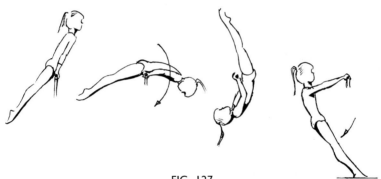

FIG. 127

The upward circle, from ground around bars, backwards   This is a more difficult move than the forward roll but is an essential skill preliminary to bar work. It can be performed on any bar or beam. On the Swedish beam, undergrasp must be used, but on a bar either grasp will be successful. Take-off can be from two feet or with one leg swinging forwards and upwards (this is the easiest). The arms must be kept bent. The legs swing up and close to the bar and until they begin to cross back over it, the head must be kept up and close in. As the legs go over the bar the body rolls round and front support is reached (fig. 128). (The teacher can aid this movement. Standing at one side of the gymnast, place one hand on the shoulder which pushes down and round while the other hand pushes under the hips.)

This can be practised also from sitting on a mat on the floor underneath a very low bar (leaving just sufficient room for the head to clear the floor). The gymnast pulls upwards to roll the body back over the low bar.

FIG. 128

Hanging on bar, travelling on hands These are strong heaving movements but quite small children can perform them if they are strong; in fact, the lighter the child the easier they are likely to find them.

Sideways travelling Facing the bar, the gymnast jumps up to hang, with the bar high enough to hang at full stretch with the feet about one foot off the ground. The hands grip in overgrasp. The body must be straight, arms shoulder width apart and shoulders down. To begin with it is advisable for the coach to start the pendulum swing of the body by gently swinging the gymnast's body sideways with a slight lifting action at each end of the swing. The gymnast should start to lift the hands slightly from the bar at the end of each swing.

When the rhythm has been established the gymnast starts to move sideways along the bar, keeping up a continuous side-to-side swinging action. If there is movement to the right, then each time the legs swing to the right the right arm reaches out in a big step; as the legs and body swing back to the left, the left arm moves to the right in a step large enough to re-establish a shoulder-width-apart position. In this way the gymnast can travel the length of a long bar. If they establish a good rhythm they can soon manage without help. They must try to keep legs together, body straight and avoid getting into a circling movement.

Backwards travelling This is similar to sideways travel but the gymnast starts at the end of the bar, back towards the direction of travel. After a forward and back swinging action has been started, one hand drops away from the bar, taking a big step backwards on the backswing. During this step the body will turn to the side of the stepping hand. As the body swings forwards again it will face to the front. On the next swing back the body will turn towards the back arm as it swings into the next step.

Vaulting Bars can also be used for vault practice, one of their advantages being that they can be adjusted more closely to the required height than a box or horse.

In some gyms the old beam saddles are still stored, often unused. They are a useful extra section of apparatus.

Bunny jumps or crouch jumps over bar   These can be made over a low bar or Swedish beam. The hands are placed along the bar-top, one in front of the other, both thumbs facing inwards towards each other. The crouch jump is performed from one side to the other with a double bounce on the floor into the jump. The hands then change places, moving further along the bar so that the second jump takes the gymnast one place further along the bar until they have travelled from one end to the other with a series of jumps side-to-side.

◼ DOUBLE BARS
The double bars can be used for a number of different heave jumps. They are useful for strength training, bar skills and vaulting.

Sheep through the gap   With two bars, one above the other; the top bar is above head height and the lower one at first is at about knee height, getting progressively higher as skill increases. The gymnast takes a few steps run to the bars, jumps to grasp the top bar in overgrasp, bends the knees to the chest to clear the lower one and then swings through the gap, stretching the legs, arching the back and aiming to land well away from the bars on the far side. The jump should be performed with the knees coming up in a tuck position. Then the legs stretch high and straight forwards, with no twisting to the side (fig. 129).

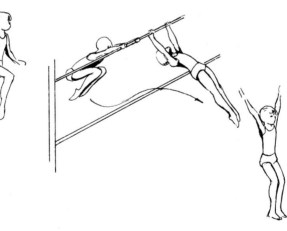

FIG. 129

Diagonal heave jump   The gymnast approaches the bars with a three step diagonal run – right-left-right, if approaching with the left shoulder to the bars. They jump to hold the top bar in overgrasp, one hand in front of the other, then swing the left leg followed by the right, high to the upper bar, pulling on the arms to swing the body high, close and parallel to it. Crossing between the bars from right to left, the gymnast aims to land well forwards from the take-off jump, right side to the bar (fig. 130).

Gate jump with half turn With three steps diagonal approach, the jump through the bars is made with one hand on the lower bar and one in overgrasp on the upper. Run with the left shoulder by the bar – right-left-right. Hold the lower bar with the left hand on top and grasp the top bar with the right hand. The legs and body should be pulled high and clear over the lower bar; then the top hand is released to allow the body to make a half turn on the left hand to land facing the starting direction (fig. 131).

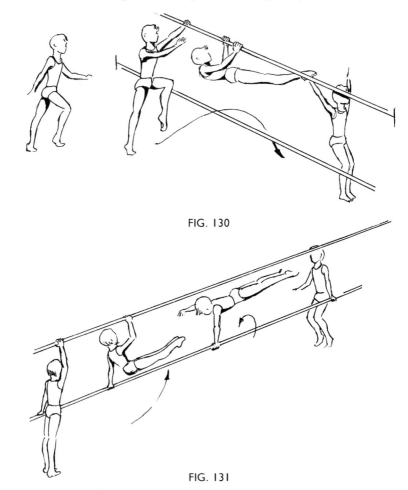

FIG. 130

FIG. 131

High crouch jump over double bar from sloping bench This takes a good deal of courage initially and will probably be performed only by the school gym-club member.

Double bars are used, one above the other, with a bench sloping up and hooked on to the lower bar. The distance apart will depend upon the height and skill of the gymnast. The height of the two bars will also depend upon skill and courage; it is better to start fairly low and build up skill. A good mattress landing area is essential here.

The gymnast takes a few steps run up the bench, uses it as a springboard at the top and double beats from it, placing both hands on the top of the upper bar, crouch jumping sideways over it.

Gate vault From front support on top of the upper of two bars, the gymnast releases one hand and leans over the bar to place the hand on the lower bar directly under the remaining hand. The body will now be sloping sideways towards the lower hand. With a strong thrust from the legs and a good push from the hands, both legs swing up and over the top bar, legs stretched and feet together, coming down to land side to the bar.

Vaults using beam saddles If beam saddles are available in a gym, they can be employed usefully as an extra vault practice. They fit across the top of a Swedish beam and can be used for squat or through vault (fig. 132). For straddle vault they are often somewhat insecure since they are high and tip forwards in use.

However, beam saddles are useful for landing practices since the bar can be adjusted to any height to give take-off from the top, and they are useful for the number of shapes of jump which can take place from the top of the saddle – star, pike, straddle, turning, etc.

FIG. 132

Rhythmic gymnastics

☐

This chapter serves as an introduction to rope, hoop and ball practices which can be fun to do in school.

Ropes and skipping

The rope can be used for skipping, swinging, throwing and jumping. It is not necessary to have handles on ropes; in fact, in rhythmic gymnastics handles are not permitted. In school many different types of rope may be used – nylon, plastic, beaded plastic, hemp, perlon. Some of these are difficult or expensive to obtain but a local yacht club may be useful in providing terylene; this should be ⅝ or ¾ inch in circumference.

The length of skipping rope is very important; standing in the middle of the rope with it under the arch of the feet and held tightly, the ends should reach the armpits (fig. 133).

FIG. 133

Since it can be performed on most flat surfaces, skipping can be practised in the gym, hall or playground, on grass or hard surfaces. It can be used in races or for display items.

Skipping is a good test of co-ordination and footwork. It is this which sometimes causes difficulty in first learning to skip and then in increasing the skills. Some early practices and skill training may be needed.

■ *PRACTICES FOR SKIPPING*
Practise bouncing on the spot, both feet together, landing each time on the balls of the feet. Don't let the heels come down to the ground. Lift the feet only high enough for a rope to pass underneath. Knees relax and bend a little each time the feet touch the ground. Rest between practices by putting the heels down to avoid strain.

SKIPPING FOR UNDER 6'S

The under 6's find skipping difficult. Fun activities will help them to learn the necessary co-ordination.

1 Two helpers hold the long rope off the ground. The child runs and does a little jump over the rope and runs on.

2 Increase the difficulty by swinging the rope. The child runs as it swings towards her and then runs out quickly.

3 Two helpers 'snake' the rope for the child to jump over and run out.

4 Standing at the side of the rope, facing one of the turners, the child learns to bounce from side to side, at first over a static rope and then over a gently swinging one.

5 Before learning to skip alone (which is difficult because the child has to learn the arm action of rope swinging as well as co-ordinating the footwork), skipping is best done with helpers turning the rope fairly slowly and evenly while the child stands in and jumps.

6 Quite young children can learn to run in and out of a rope being turned for them. Watch the rope at the top point, then run fast in and out again before the rope catches up.

If the child cannot manage the timing of this alone, they can be helped by running in holding the hand of an older child.

7 When the child first learns to skip alone the rope should be held in a relaxed grip so that it will rotate in the hands. This should be done with the arms well extended. They will usually find it easiest to skip forwards first because they can see the rope coming.

To help the timing of skipping alone, the child can learn to swing the rope at the side of the body. First with the right hand and then with the left, practise swinging the rope in a circle so that it just touches the ground. The lower arm makes the first circle and after that it is almost entirely a wrist action. When this has been mastered with both hands, add a jump so that as the rope hits the ground, the gymnast does a small upward jump (fig. 134). This should be practised on both sides and then put together with the gymnast in the middle skipping forwards.

SKIPPING FOR 6-10 YEAR OLDS

At first the skipper will skip very slowly and with a jerky action. It is easiest to learn skipping with a bounce in between each step at first, and only add continuous skipping when this skill has been mastered smoothly. The rope may bang on the floor to begin with and then must be corrected so that the rope only just clears the ground.

The child should begin to make the skipping co-ordinated and flowing. It may be a good idea to introduce skipping to music now. The arms should

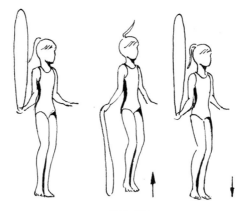

FIG. 134

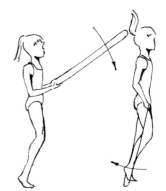

FIG. 135

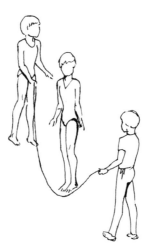

FIG. 136

be stretched well away from the body and the rope should not be heard to touch the ground (fig. 135). Skipping forwards, backwards and sideways can be introduced as skill increases.

Changes of rhythm should be introduced – slow, medium and fast, single and double skipping.

Movement on the spot and in patterns round the room, combinations of speed, travelling and steps can now become more intricate and the gymnast can begin to work out simple sequences. When first putting steps in a routine, it is as well to do each step four times.

▮ SKIPPING RHYMES AND JINGLES

Many of the old skipping jingles are still enjoyed by children today. Some have been updated, many retain part or all of the words and actions used in playgrounds for years. All are good practice for speed or rhythm changes and for co-ordination skills.

1   Done singly or with two helpers turning (fig. 136). Skippers and helpers chant.

> *Mother's in the kitchen*
> *Doing a bit of stitching*
> *How many stitches*
> *Can she do?*
> [fast turning without bounce]
> *One, two, three* [etc. until 'out']

2   Singly or with helpers. All chant (with a bounce).

> *Sea shells, cockle shells*
> *Eavie, Ivy, Over*
> *Here comes the teacher, with a big black stick*
> *Have you done your Arithmetic?*
>
> *How many pages have you done?*
> [fast without a bounce]
> *One, two, three* [etc.]

3   With two helpers turning the rope. Each line has an action to be performed by the skipper.

> *Teddy Bear, Teddy Bear, turn around*
> *Teddy Bear, Teddy Bear, touch the ground*
> *Teddy Bear, Teddy Bear, do high kicks*
> *Teddy Bear, Teddy Bear, show your knicks*
> *Teddy Bear, Teddy Bear, go upstairs*
> *Teddy Bear, Teddy Bear, say your prayers*
> *Teddy Bear, Teddy Bear, turn out the light*
> *Teddy Bear, Teddy Bear, spell Goodnight*
> [fast turning]
> *G-O-O-D-N-I-G-H-T*

4   A ring of children (about five or six), one in the middle skipping alone. He/she chants.

> *I like coffee*
> *I like tea*
> *I'd like (Sarah) in with me*
> [calls her friend in to skip with her: then after a number
> of times together]
> *I hate coffee*
> *I hate tea*
> *I hate Sarah in with me*

Sarah runs out and another is called in. After several turns or if the skipping fails, another is chosen to be the caller.

5   Two helpers turning the rope, a line of skippers waiting to run in on the side facing the rope as it comes down (fig. 137). Call child's name – *Under the moon – Mary*. Mary has to run in as the rope is at the top, skip once, and out, then line up on the other side. When all the line have crossed successfully they are called back one by one – *Over the stars – Mandy*. They run in, waiting for the rope to come low on the ground, jump over it and skip once, then run out (much more difficult) (fig. 138). This can be an elimination game; anyone failing is out.

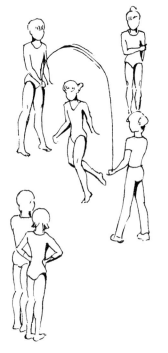

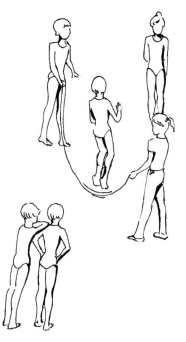

FIG. 137   FIG. 138

■SKIPPING STEPS AND PATTERNS FOR OVER 10'S

Many steps and rhythm changes can be taught with a skipping rope. Skipping with a rebound bounce is called 'half time', the fast skipping which one sees boxers doing is called 'full time' and two turns of the rope under the feet is 'doubles'.

1 Skipping on one foot then the other. Make a pattern of steps – four on the left, four on the right, four together.

2 Side step. Stand on a line, facing along the line. Bounce first step on the line, second step with left foot tapping to the left of the line, third step bounce on the line again, fourth step with the right foot to the right (fig. 139). Repeat. (A more advanced side step is to leave out the bounce on the line and skip from side to side.)

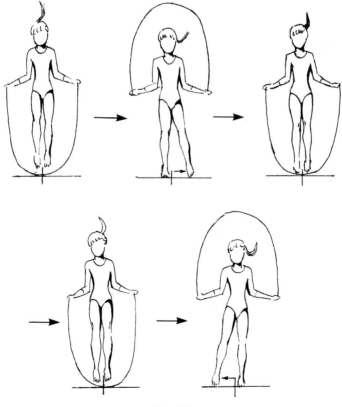

FIG. 139

3 Side swing. Not all skipping depends only upon changes of step; it may also have the addition of rope swinging and body movement (fig. 140).

   a Skip once with the rope turning forwards.
   b After landing, the rope swings upwards and then on the

downward swing the rope is taken to the right side of the body and circled forwards, left arm across the body.

c As the rope swings down again, the left hand moves back to the left of the body and a normal swing and step takes place.

d This is then repeated to the left, right hand moving across.

It is advisable to practise these rope swings without skipping at first; when the swings are correct add the jumps. In rhythmic gymnastics this is a figure

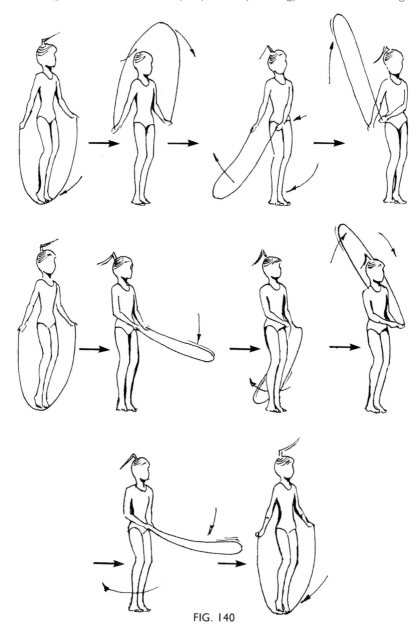

FIG. 140

of eight and should have added to it a body wave either following the line of the rope or away from it. Also added can be a circle of the rope overhead, accompanied by a body wave. These moves can be done by transferring the rope first to one hand and then to the other instead of crossing the arms over the body.

4 Forward arm cross. On the first turn of the rope bounce with the feet together. The rope continues up and overhead. As it swings down the arms are crossed one over the other. The arms cross at the elbows and the hands point outwards. Jump over the rope while the arms are still crossed. The rope continues upwards, arms still crossed, but as it descends the arms are quickly uncrossed. A normal skip then follows (fig. 141). This can be repeated in various patterns – one plain, one cross; two plain, one cross, etc.

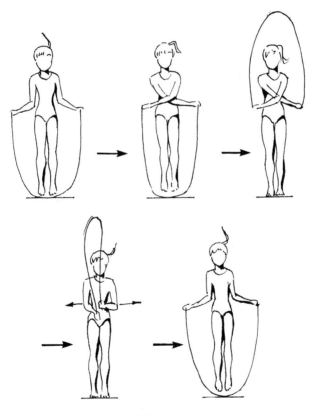

FIG. 141

5 Backward cross. As above but with the rope turned backwards.

6 Now begin to add forward, backward and sideways movement to your skipping. Skip once feet together; next step, skip on the left and at the same time hop forwards, right knee bent and right foot to the back of the left knee. Repeat with a two-foot bounce and then a hop forwards right.

7 Double skipping (fig. 142). This is skipping performed with two turns of the rope to one jump (often called 'bumps' by children). The rope must be turned very fast, with a wrist action rather than with the arm. The arms are kept fairly straight and only lifted a little way from the body, the wrist action initiating the fast rope turn. It is this fast turn, rather than a high jump, which aids this double skip. This skill is best performed alternating with single skipping. Try 1, 2, 3, single jumps followed by a double. Double skips can also be made with crossed arms.

FIG. 142

■ *OTHER MOVEMENTS WITH THE ROPE*

Rhythmic gymnastics identify three planes of movement. These are areas of space round the body through which the body can move or the apparatus can swing (fig. 143).

1 The wheel plane: the area at the side of the body through which the apparatus can swing forwards or backwards vertically.
2 The door plane: the area in front of the body through which a side-to-side swing may be performed.
3 The table plane: the flat area round the body through which turning swings are performed.

The gymnast should practise swinging the rope in all these planes, combining the swings with body waves and turns. (The rope is not the easiest apparatus with which to illustrate these planes because it tends to kink and must be kept free and continuously moving.)

Jumps Most of the basic jumps used in artistic gymnastics can also be performed in rope work (fig. 144).

Folded rope The rope can also be used folded – double, treble and even in four. Folded, the rope can be jumped over, used to support the free leg in balance, thrown and re-caught or thrown to a partner in pairs work.

Wrap The rope can be swung so that it wraps around a part of the body.

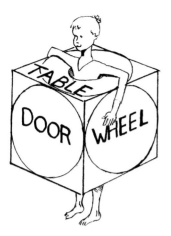

FIG. 143

Split leap

Komat (cat jump)

Tuck jump

Stag leap

Pike

Scissor

FIG. 144

Hold the rope at each end. Swing it to the right, keeping the right arm stretched and the left arm across the body. Continue to swing the rope, circling backwards, and it will wrap around the arm (fig. 145). Circle the rope forwards and it will unwind.

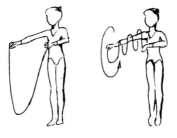

FIG. 145

Children of all ages will manage these basic rope movements and, given time to experiment, they will soon devise moves of their own. From these moves, sequences can be worked, music used, skips, jumps, body waves and balances combined in an interesting introduction to rhythmic gymnastics.

When a large class is working pairs work can be introduced - skipping in pairs with one rope; follow my leader, each with a rope, working facing each other with two ropes, mirroring the partner's moves; working in unison with a partner following moves in sequence or working in canon, one performing a short series, followed exactly by the partner, or each member of the group, in turn.

Rope relay race This exercise works well in a warm-up and also makes an exciting finish to a session. Two or more teams line up, in pairs, behind a start line (fig. 146). A length of rope is on the floor in front of each team, behind another line and the length of the gym in front of the teams. The front

FIG. 146

pair in each line run up to their rope, pick it up at each end and drag it back along the ground between them. As they reach the team, being careful to run level with each other, the whole team in turn jumps over the rope as it reaches them. Then the team ducks down as the rope is carried back overhead, carried to the front of the room and placed back on the ground, behind the line. (Any team with part of the rope on or over the line is sent back to correct it.) The pair who have completed their turn now run back to touch the next pair and take their place at the back of the team. The race finishes when the first and last pairs are back in their original start positions and the rope is correctly in place.

Ball handling

The balls used for rhythmic gymnastics are 18–20 cm (7–8 in) in diameter, with a minimum weight of 400 g (14 oz). In the school situation, however, particularly with the younger children, it is important to become familiar with balls of tennis ball size, up to netball/football size and weight. The air-flow type of ball can also be useful, as can be the sponge ball, particularly if the room is crowded or there are dangerous lights or windows.

Rolling, bouncing, throwing, catching and swinging, while controlling the ball, are all moves to be learned and practised. Ball skills are important for many games as well as rhythmic gymnastics and are often better mastered in the gym than on a cold playing field.

In games playing, accuracy of catching, passing, receiving and intercepting are paramount. In gymnastics, throwing and catching in pairs and groups is vital; also, solo work which mainly requires elegant throwing and re-catching, bouncing, rolling, combined with body waves and circles, leaps and jumps, and balances. Great ball control is required, allied to the ability to work equally well with left and right hand and to demonstrate continuous movement either with body waves or dance, leaps and balances.

■ *UNDER 6'S*

It is important that the under 6's learn to throw and catch first because their throwing is often wild and inaccurate. At first it is best if the teacher or helpers do the throwing, teaching the child to catch. *Watch the ball* is a favourite teaching point, but often leads to the child watching the ball in the teacher's hand as it leaves and then ceasing to follow the flight of the ball. *Watch it right into your hands* seems to have better results. The child should be taught to stand facing the thrower, one foot slightly in front of the other, hands cupped ready to receive the ball, with the palms up. As the ball reaches the hands they should be gathered softly into the body, pulling the ball in, fingers closely round or on to the ball. Later the child must learn to catch inaccurately thrown balls into the hands and with either left or right hand only.

When the child has learnt to catch a ball thrown by the coach, move on to throwing and catching in two's and solo. There are many different throws used in games playing, where the aim is usually to get the ball accurately to another team member or to field a ball and throw back with a long overarm throw. Here, as long as the result is achieved, the style of throw is unimportant. This is not the case in gymnastics, where throwing and catching *must* be aesthetically pleasing. The ball must be thrown and caught smoothly with a continuous movement. Body movements such as waves, bends, rolls and jumps must be included while the ball is in the air. Any ball handling practices will improve a child's repertoire of skills.

■ OLDER CHILDREN

1 Throw against a wall and catch the return.

2 Throw and turn round before catching.

3 Throw, touch the ground before the catch.

4 Throw, hit the wall, let the ball bounce before catching.

5 Throw, hit the wall, kick one leg over as it bounces and catch.

6 As above, partner throwing for the other gymnast to catch.

7 Target practice, throwing against a target marked on the wall (fig. 147).

All these practices are to be performed with either the left or the right hand.

■ BOUNCING

Bouncing a ball in gymnastics is not the same as in games playing. Here, as for example in basketball, the aim is to keep control of the ball for as long as possible, or in netball to give a bounce pass. In gymnastics the ball should be well away from the body as it is bounced, with a well extended arm to give an elegant line and to allow time for other movements to take place.

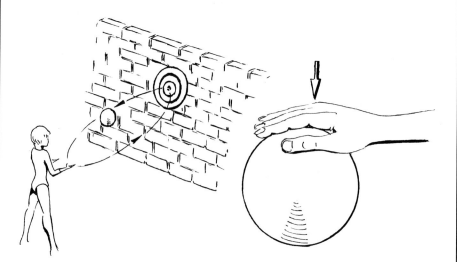

FIG. 147   FIG. 148

In gymnastic bouncing the ball must be well controlled. It should not be hit with a flat hand, which leads to noisy bouncing, but should be pressed into the floor by the fingers pressing downwards, with the hand and wrist flexible (fig. 148).

At first the young child will only manage bounce and catch with both hands but will soon manage continuous bouncing with either hand singly.

■ *MUSIC*

Bouncing to music adds interest and is a good way of starting the young child working with music. Variety can be introduced with high, medium and low bouncing. With the use of suitable music, different speeds and rhythms of bouncing can be introduced.

Bouncing and catching in pairs to music is also a valuable practice (fig. 149). As the skill increases, so other movements can be added to the bouncing and catching – body waves and turns, runs and jumps and rolls.

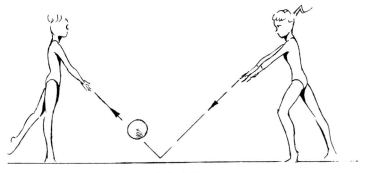

FIG. 149

■ *ROLLING*

This is another important part of work with the ball. The easiest roll to be taught to the young gymnast is along the floor. This should be a smooth action and the ball should flow freely off the finger-tips without interruption, jerking or bouncing. Rolling along the floor requires the gymnast to get down close to the floor and release the ball smoothly from the palm of the hand and off the finger-tips. This must entail an elegant low starting position of the body and a well stretched arm and hand.

Working with a partner, the partner collects the rolled ball with the back of the hand to the floor and the ball is allowed to run up the fingers on to the hand (fig. 150). Later the gymnast can collect his/her own rolled ball, running to overtake it, turning to collect.

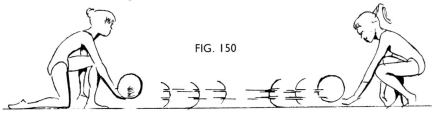

FIG. 150

MORE ADVANCED SKILLS

When proficiency in ball control has been achieved, more innovative and advanced work can be attempted. The ball should always be caught on a flat hand, the fingers must never grip the ball, nor may it be hugged to the body or tucked in against the lower arm. The backs of the hand can be used to catch, as can the upper arm, between the arms held above and behind the head, and the back of the neck.

When throwing there are three points of release.

1 To gain height and length, the ball should be thrown with a strong arm swing, arm and wrist well stretched at about shoulder height. This will be used when throwing to a partner or for a forward throw to allow movement along the floor to catch up with the ball.

2 To throw high above the head, the point of release is higher, well directed above the head.

3 To throw behind the head, the arm and hand must swing up and above and behind the head to project the ball high and backwards. The same points of release are used when projecting other rhythmic apparatus, such as the hoop.

TRAVELLING WITH THE BALL

The rhythmic exercise must exhibit good movement across the floor, showing interesting choreography and pattern. This may be achieved by throwing or bouncing the ball ahead of the gymnast to give time and space for rolls and jumps or dance to take place as the ball is released before being re-caught. A valuable practice for this is to work with a partner to judge exactly how hard and far the ball needs to travel for the gymnast to have time and room to perform the required move before attempting to re-catch it. The first gymnast pushes the ball forwards with a long bounce or a throw for the partner to catch and then sees where they will finish when performing the gymnastic move. By getting the partner to stand at the finishing spot, the gymnast can then judge and practise how to throw or bounce the ball to the exact spot required.

Hoops

The gymnastic hoop should be hip height when standing at the side of the gymnast. Hoops used in school may be made of wood, but they are more often made of plastic. The surface may be round or flat edged. Rhythmic gymnasts often bind their hoops with coloured tape to complement their leotards and add to the aesthetic appearance of their performance.

When holding the hoop the grip will usually be light, with either over or undergrasp, but at times the hoop needs to be more firmly gripped with one or two hands. For some games and skills it will often need to be held quite firmly.

■ HOOP GAMES AND RACES

I Teams of racers bowl their hoops from one end of the room to the other, running with the hoop and propelling it with a flat hand for the second runner in the team to collect and return, bowling to runner three.

2 The same relay can be made more skilful by placing skittles or other objects down the track which must be slalomed around. (When the players become skilful they can be made to return to the start if either their hoop falls flat or they have to hold on to it to steer or prevent it from falling.)

3 Learn to skip on the spot in a hoop, turning the hoop forwards (fig. 151). Then try skipping in the hoop while running forwards (fig. 152). Relay races as above can then be devised, skipping in the hoop instead of bowling it.

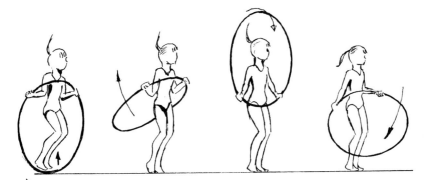

FIG. 151

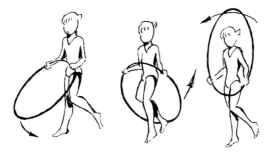

FIG. 152

4 Star relay. This combines bringing the hoop up the body, down to the feet and bowling. Teams stand in four lines in a star shape, a hoop with the four team leaders at the front of each line. They step into the hoop and bring it up the body and over the head, hand it back to the child behind, who puts it over the head, down the body and steps out. When it reaches the last in the line they put it over the head or over the feet (whichever alternate it is) and then bowl it right round the outside of the circle until they get back to their own line. Then they cut in front and hand on to the second player who starts by stepping into the hoop and bringing it up the body and over the head.

5 Hoop jump relay (fig. 153). Teams line up in two's, the first two in each team running up to a line in the front of the room behind which a hoop is placed on the floor. They pick up the hoop between them and, carrying it low and flat to the ground, run back with it to the team. Each pair must then jump into and out of the hoop on the other side. When the carriers get to the end of the line, the line ducks and they carry it overhead to the front of the room, putting it down behind the starting line and then running back to touch the next two in the line who run for the hoop. The runners who have finished go to the back of the line. The race ends when all the runners are back in their starting place, sitting down, and the hoop is back in its starting position.

FIG. 153

6 The same race can be played with the gymnasts crawling through the hoop instead of jumping in and out of it.

7 Zig-zag bowling relay (fig. 154). (This race is best played with teams of an uneven number.) Teams stand in two's, facing each other in alternate spaces, each with a chalk mark showing their place. Number one bowls the hoop diagonally across to number two and so on down the line, until the last player has the hoop (e.g. number 5 or 7 or 9). Last players from *both* sides then run to the first places in the line (e.g. 9–1, 8–2) and everyone moves down one place. Number nine then starts the bowling action.

If the hoop fails to cross the line so that the catcher can reach it without stepping over the line, the bowler must chase it, return to her place and bowl again.

Instead of running back with the hoop, the players may be made to bowl it, skip in it, or throw and catch while on the run.

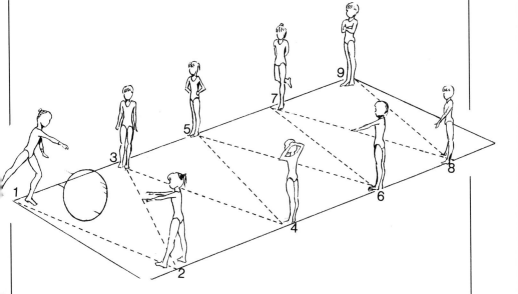

FIG. 154

▓ *FUN WITH HOOPS IN PAIRS*

1 One partner rolls the hoop and the other gymnast star or straddle jumps over the hoop as it rolls towards them (fig. 155). Then try jumping over, turning quickly on landing and catching, then re-rolling to the first gymnast.

2 Partner rolls the hoop and second gymnast quickly passes through it as it rolls past.

FIG. 155

3 Throwing and catching the hoop with a forward and upward throw to a partner. Practise throwing and catching left- and right-handed.

4 Standing side by side, one throws the hoop forwards and upwards while partner rolls forwards, stands and catches (fig. 156). This can also be performed with jumps instead of rolls.

FIG. 156

▓PRACTICES WITH A HOOP EACH

1 Hula hoop (fig. 157). Circling the hoop around different parts of the body, e.g. wrist, arm, neck, ankle.

2 Reverse roll (fig. 158). This is made by putting back-spin on to the hoop. The arm swings strongly forwards to roll the hoop but as it is about to leave the hand the wrist jerks up and back, applying back-spin and causing the hoop to travel first forwards and then back to the sender. When this has been perfected the gymnast can perform other moves before the hoop returns, such as balances, spins, body waves or jumps.

3 Throw the hoop forwards and upwards and run and leap before re-catching.

4 Swinging the hoop on different parts of the body. The hoop can be made to swing on foot, ankle, hand, wrist, neck, and with the body in various starting positions. This should be made to look as elegant as possible: the hand should be held with the arm stretched, a slight up-and-down and rotary movement rotating the hoop on a softly held hand. On the foot or ankle the feet should be shown to be well stretched. Once the skill has been mastered, other moves should be added such as balances on the toes or running steps.

5 As with the swings described in the rope section, movement can take place in the wheel, table and window planes.

Both undergrasp and overgrasp may be used when working with the hoop. For rotation movements the hoop rests on the hand in undergrasp, hand and fingers well extended and the hoop controlled and circling between the thumb and first finger. In overgrasp, the fingers are placed over the rim of the hoop but the first finger runs along the rim to give strength and control. This is the grip used to cause the hoop to roll back towards the gymnast in the boomerang roll.

When these basic moves have been perfected, the gymnast, either solo or with a partner, can become much more innovative in adding jumps, dance, body moves, spins and throws to the sequence of movements, trying all the time to provide continuous, smooth movement, interesting shapes and patterns, musical interpretation and cleanly performed skills. Body waves can add interest and elegance to most rhythmic throwing and catching (fig. 159).

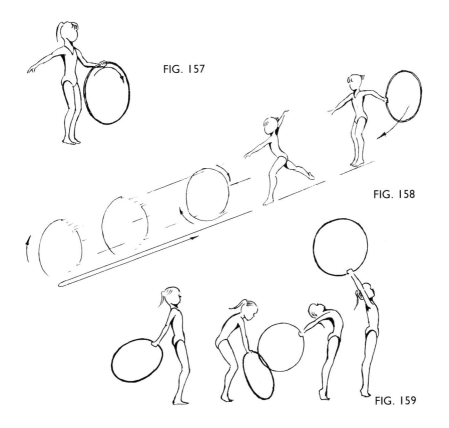

FIG. 157

FIG. 158

FIG. 159

Sports acrobatics

□

There is unlimited scope for gymnastic activities based on partner balances. Devise yourself a sequence based on simple pair balances, linked together with pleasing choreography, add some tumbles, and you have taken your first steps into sports acrobatics.

The British Schools National Sports Acrobatics Championships have categories catering for girls' pairs, boys' pairs and mixed pairs, all at under 11, under 13 and under 18 age groups.

Besides giving the participants a great deal of enjoyment, pairs and group balancing challenges the imagination and resourcefulness of children. There is frequently more than one method of achieving a balance and discovering an ingenious one can be a task set by the teacher. Children will need to make decisions based on difference in weight, strength and ability. Co-operation is essential to successful balances. Moving into and out of a balance is as important as the balance itself and should be done with grace and elegance. The scope of pairs balancing is infinite and only a few of the many possibilities are shown in figs 160–163.

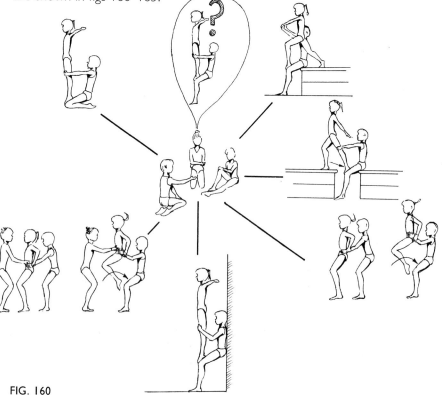

FIG. 160

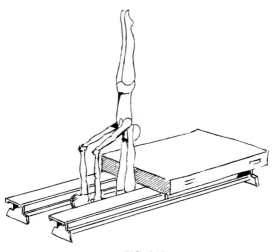

FIG. 161

Working in three's, four's, five's and so on does not necessarily mean more difficult work; indeed, a tableau involving many children can be devised by simply joining together different pairs balances. The Schools Championships have a category for groups of six children. Each group at one point in their routine must show a group balance. All of the balances illustrated in figs 166–168 (pages 116-9) have been demonstrated by participating schools and show how diverse and imaginative teams can be.

An examination of the illustrations will show clearly which are the more difficult undertakings. At its simplest, a tableau can be a pleasing arrangement of postures (fig. 167), or dramatic and difficult as in fig. 168 on page 119. A word of caution here: balances which go three and four persons high are difficult and should only be attempted by very experienced groups, always under supervision with spotters standing by.

One of the most popular pairs balances is the one shown in fig. 163. It is sometimes called 'knee-and-shoulder balance' and though not particularly easy to set up, once positioned it becomes very stable. The secret is to establish a vertical line through the balancer's body and the arms of the bearer. A common mistake is attempting to maintain a balance in the position shown with a cross. Important to the success of most balances is 'locking out'; that is, making sure supporting arms and legs are perfectly straight.

The pairs balances illustrated can be divided into three groups, the simplest being those combinations where both participants have contact with the floor. Though easier to perform, this type can look very pleasing as part of a routine or larger tableau. A second group, usually harder to execute, are those where one of the pair has wide base contact with the ground and supports the other in a balance. A third group involve balance on a small base; these rely on counter-balancing of weight to give stability. Children gain considerable satisfaction from achieving these, probably because of the degree of co-operation required.

FIG. 162

A sensible use of matting and other apparatus will make those balances which at first seem precarious much safer in the learning stages. The arrangement shown in fig. 161 can be used for many combinations, giving the balancer on top a chance to roll out on to the matting in the event of an over-balance or a collapse on the part of the bearer.

Those pairs balances where the bearer takes the hands away from the balancer can be made with hand contact until the balance is sure. A third person can be most useful in the early stages, lending a helping hand to lift or hold the piece steady until it is set up.

Balances involving more than two people are not necessarily harder than pairs; in fact, some can be broad based and stable, such as the traditional pyramid. Narrow based balances, where the bearer is standing and supporting two or more others in counter-balance, are normally harder, but with planning and practice they can be achieved by the more able.

Making shapes and balances in pairs or groups can be great fun for the participants and, indeed, any onlookers. The work is easily adapted to displays, lending itself to musical accompaniment and choreography.

FIG. 162

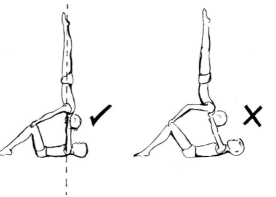

FIG. 163

FIG. 164

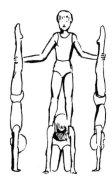

FIG. 165

FIG. 166

FIG. 166

FIG. 166

FIG. 166

FIG. 167

FIG. 168

Activities for school and display

These activities are good for displays, as a part of warm-up, or as light relief in a strengthening programme.

■ BREAST STROKE
The pair progress along the floor with the lower gymnast bending and stretching the legs, pushing the body forwards with the arms. The top gymnast assists the move, lifting and bending backwards with the body, swimming with the arms (fig. 169).

FIG. 169

■ BEETLE RIDE
Gymnast in support position moves forwards on hands and feet. Lower one hangs on with feet locked round the waist and hands round the lower back (fig. 170).

■ BEETLE RACE
Beetle ride can be used as a team race. First pair move down a long mat, cross a line and roll over so that they change positions with each other, returning back down the mat until the next pair in the line is touched and take their place (fig. 171).

FIG. 170   FIG. 171

JUMPS AND ROLLS IN THREE'S

Three gymnasts stand about two paces apart as *A B C* in fig. 172. *A* starts with a tight forward roll under the legs of *B*. *B* does a straddle jump upwards and forwards over *A*. *C* pauses, then does a tight forward roll under *A* who has now come up from the roll into a forward and upward straddle jump. *A* and *B* then jump-turn to face the opposite way to continue rolling and jumping alternately, in the new direction.

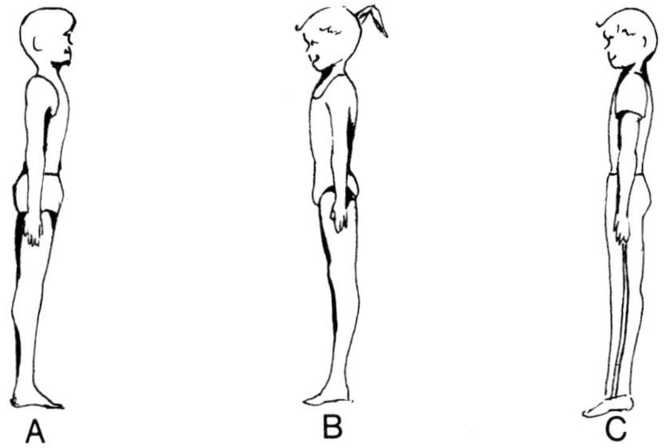

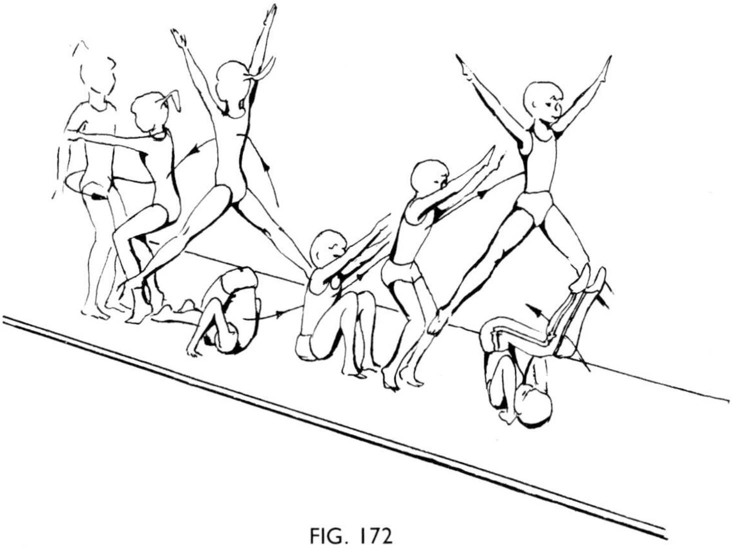

FIG. 172

LIFTING SCALES

Gymnasts take up a wheelbarrow position but with the hands of the lifter high up the waist of the partner to be raised. The lifting gymnast then helps the partner to rise with a strong back action, arms out to the side. When a good balance has been achieved, the support can lean backwards and raise the arms, counter-balancing the partner who clasps their feet together (fig. 173).

FIG. 173

■ LINKED-ARM PUSH-UP

(Useful as a leg strengthening exercise.) Gymnasts sit back to back, arms linked and legs bent. Pushing flat backs against each other, they straighten legs to stand (fig. 174a). This can also be done in groups of three or four (fig. 174b).

FIG. 174a   FIG. 174b

■ ELEPHANT WALK

In pairs. The smaller gymnast jumps on to the waist of the larger one, locking ankles together at the back of the waist. This gymnast then drops back to the floor, on to the hands and walks through the support's legs. The support then bends forwards and places their hands on the floor. The supported gymnast then can walk on their hands. But this gives the elephant six legs, so it is better to place the hands on the back of the ankles of the support and the elephant can then walk forwards, in the direction of the support's head (fig. 175).

FIG. 175

▨ CENTIPEDE

Gymnasts sit between the straddled legs of the gymnast behind. The front one turns over on all fours, the second turns over and puts their feet clasped on the back of the one behind, followed by each one in the line in turn. When the centipede has formed it moves forwards, the gymnasts rolling out with a forward roll, one after the other (fig. 176).

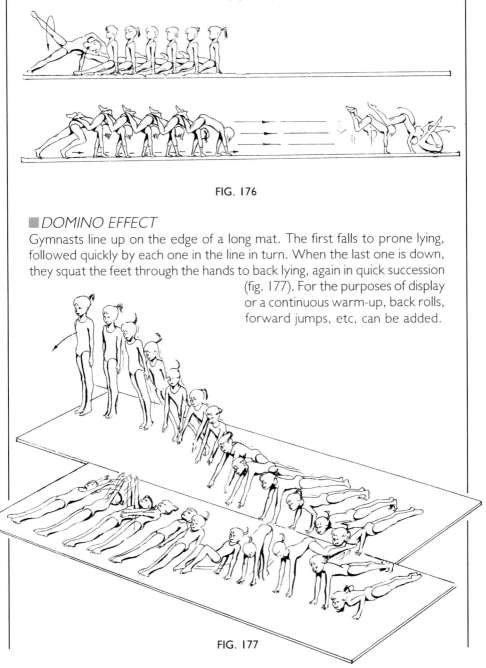

FIG. 176

▨ DOMINO EFFECT

Gymnasts line up on the edge of a long mat. The first falls to prone lying, followed quickly by each one in the line in turn. When the last one is down, they squat the feet through the hands to back lying, again in quick succession (fig. 177). For the purposes of display or a continuous warm-up, back rolls, forward jumps, etc, can be added.

FIG. 177

Competitive gymnastics

☐

Gymnastics lend themselves to competition because they can be organised to include almost any age or level of ability.

The FIG, the body that governs all international gymnastics, publishes a new 'Code of Points' after each Olympic Games; the work of all national gymnasts is based on this. Also published is a 'world set' exercise on each piece of apparatus, which must be learned and performed at all the major world competitions.

Competitions for novices can be organised with very simple set or voluntary rules, suitable for any age or standard. Championships within the school, between classes or houses, or inter-school competitions can be set up.

The British Schools Gymnastic Association (BSGA) has run a most successful competition, now in its eighteenth year, which attracts hundreds of school teams each year. Teams of under 11 and under 16 girls or boys all from the same school, compete in teams of five or six, with five scores to count. Each member of the team performs a voluntary floor sequence, lasting up to forty seconds. The sequence must contain six moves from the BAGA Awards. Each move is worth 0.5, so as long as the six moves are performed, the score starts at 3.0.

The moves are then linked by dance and jumps and should exhibit good changes of floor pattern, tempo and rhythm – this part is worth two marks. Four marks are given for execution of the skills and movement pattern. One mark is given for general impression.

Each gymnast then has two attempts at any vault from the Award scheme. These are tariffed according to difficulty; thus an attempt at squat on, jump off (candle jump) will only start at 2.0, while a straddle vault lengthwise (long fly) starts at 4.0. Marks are then awarded for flight (1.5), shape (2.0) and flight off (2.5).

The third part of the competition is a synchronised group sequence, performed by all members of the team, requiring twelve moves from the BAGA Awards Charts (moves can be repeated once to make twelve, i.e. six moves repeated once each) and these must be linked by dance and interesting patterns. The sequence is performed to music and the score is out of 30. Score cards for this competition are thus:

Individual floor		Individual vault		Group sequence	
Six moves	3.0	Tariff of vault (up to)	4.0	Synchronisation	5.0
Dance, links, pattern	2.0	Flight on	1.5	Composition	5.0
Execution	4.0	Flight off	2.5	Execution	15.0
General impression	1.0	Shape	2.0	Musical interpretation/	
				general impression	5.0
	10.0		10.0		
					30.0

A similar competition, on floor and vault only, is also run by the BSGA, again for school teams of six competitors, under 11 or under 18. The choice of moves or vaults which may be included is increased for this competition: moves from the Award scheme plus a number of moves and vaults listed. The under 18 age range is valuable because it gives girls and boys who have not been able to keep up full competitive gymnastics, the chance to continue participation. This competition is quite within the capability of school gym-clubs.

For a novice group, a simple competition can be composed with each gymnast performing the same set routine. To encourage some individuality and widen the scores, jumps and dance links can be left to the individual. This need not be on a full floor square, which is 12 m × 12 m, but can be on a strip of mats which is likely to suit primary schools, who may only work on a small area. An example of such might be as follows.

Floor sequence: forward roll to standing, any high jump, one or two steps into a cartwheel; two teddy bear rolls (straddle rolls), backward roll to stand, quarter-turn jump to face starting position; any balance position, held for three seconds, return to start with any combination of running, dance steps, jumps.

3 marks (0.5 each) for roll, cartwheel, teddy bears, back roll, quarter-turn jump, balance. 2.5 marks for linkage – running, dancing and jumps. 4.0 marks for execution. 0.5 marks for neatness and appearance of gymnast.

Vault: squat jump on to a box 103 cm high. Immediate high jump off. Marked out of 10.

Planning a competition

Agree and print the competition format and rules   Not only give the content required and marks to be awarded, but consider penalties which may need to be deducted – e.g. 0.2 overtime or undertime, 0.5 fall, 0.3 each set move omitted. Publish these.

Book the venue   Make sure the required apparatus is available, plus facilities for spectators.

Arrange judges and officials If there are two judges per piece, their scores are averaged. If four can judge each piece, the top and bottom marks should be crossed out and the middle two averaged, e.g. 8.3, 8.5, 8.8, 8.6 – 8.3 and 8.8 are crossed out and 8.5 and 8.6 are averaged = 8.55.

Scores Have a method of showing or announcing scores.

Recorders Have runners taking judges' scores to the recorder, who records individual and team totals.

Timekeeper Stopwatch and official are required for noting time and any deductions to be made for time faults.

Apparatus Check that the required apparatus is out and positioned safely. Check mats are suitable.

Public address Make sure announcements and music can be amplified. Music, if used, should be presented by the gymnast at the start of a clean tape, named and numbered.

Announcer Responsible for giving out scores and notices.

Floor manager Responsible for keeping the competition moving smoothly and to time.

Numbers For each gymnast to hold up so that judges can identify the gymnast on their notes.

Rules Provide a copy of rules and format for each judge.

Programme and tickets These will be required for larger competitions, where spectators and entry money are expected.

Sports acrobatics

Similar competitions can be based on sports acrobatics. British schools run a Sports Acro competition in tumbling, pairs work and group sequence. The competition is run on a regional basis in the first rounds, with school pairs or groups and individual tumblers competing to represent their regions in the national finals. Age groups are under 11, under 13 and under 18.

The pairs balances are taken from the Midland Bank Award Scheme for sports acrobatics.

The group sequence is performed by six competitors from the same school, who each perform the same four agilities and three pair balances from the charts. The whole must be linked by dance and jumps and at some point in the sequence there must be a mass balance involving all members of the team.

Similar competitions can be arranged at school or inter-school level, the standard of the competition being set by the difficulty of the balances and agilities selected.

Rhythmic gymnastics

Similar competitions can be arranged in rhythmic gymnastics. These can consist of individual work on any of the apparatus used. The competition can be in pairs or trios or in groups. The BSGA competition requires a team of four, one with a sequence with hoop, one with rope, one with ribbon and one with ball. Many variations of this format can be devised to suit the competition.

The value of competitive gymnastics

Competitive gymnastics form a valuable addition to the normal school gymnastics lesson. It is a spur and a motivation for the school gym-club and offers an opportunity for great achievement to the talented and dedicated child. Competition provides experience in winning, losing, fair play, honesty and disciplined behaviour.

Since the age of competitive gymnasts is among the lowest in sport, many school children are offered the opportunity of friendly or full international events at home or abroad, giving valuable life experiences through travel, being hosted in foreign homes, mixing with many nationalities at events such as gymnastraedas (for recreational gymnasts), the World School games (confined to national teams of school gymnasts), and club, regional or national teams.

Opportunities for the older, non-competitive gymnast

Girls and boys showing an interest in gymnastics but not wishing to compete can be offered many ways of helping school and community. At the age of fifteen, the interested ex-gymnast can take a course and exam to qualify as an assistant club coach. They cannot hold this qualification until they are sixteen and are then qualified to assist at school or club training sessions, but only in the presence of a qualified coach/teacher.

Also at sixteen, they may attend a course to qualify as a club judge, taking a theory and a practical exam which qualifies them to judge within a region at low level competitions.

Competition organisers are always requiring help with jobs such as scorers, computer scorers, timekeepers, recorders, music operators. The older pupil can give and gain valuable experience here, while the youngest can enjoy the responsibility of being a runner or score-board operator.

Beyond this, opportunities are offered to school leavers with sound gymnastic knowledge and coaching qualifications, in the leisure industry and private clubs.

Index